Tips and Tricks in

OUTDOOR EDUCATION

Approaches to Providing Children with Educational Experiences
in the Outdoors

Fifth Edition

Tips and Tricks in
OUTDOOR EDUCATION

Approaches to Providing Children with Educational Experiences
in the Outdoors

Prepared by

Members of the
Faculty in Outdoor Teacher Education
The Lorado Taft Field Campus of
Northern Illinois University

Edited by

Malcolm D. Swan, Professor Emeritis
Faculty in Outdoor Teacher Education

 **INTERSTATE PUBLISHERS, INC.**

Danville, Illinois

Tips and Tricks in

OUTDOOR EDUCATION

Fifth Edition

Library of Congress Catalog Card No. 93-77762

ISBN 0-8134-2954-4

1 2 3
4 5 6
7 8 9

Order from

INTERSTATE PUBLISHERS, INC.

510 North Vermilion Street
P.O. Box 50
Danville, IL 61834-0050

Phone: (800) 843-4774
  Fax: (217) 446-9706

Preface

Some time ago, members of what is now Northern Illinois University's Faculty in Outdoor Teacher Education (The Lorado Taft Field Campus) mimeographed an assortment of guides, plans, ideas, and suggestions that they believed would be helpful to persons wanting to provide children with educational experiences outdoors. This *Instructional Materials Packet* became quite popular. Hence, a decision was made to revise and enlarge the packet and to publish it in book form. The resulting *Tips and Tricks in Outdoor Education* also met with a good reception, and educators have found the first four editions to be valuable in providing students with outdoor/environmental education experiences. Hopefully they will find this fifth edition even more useful.

While Malcolm D. Swan gave leadership for all editions, each contributor's initials appear in the Table of Contents after the title of his or her work. Persons responsible for the various areas are listed as compilers. Contributors are:

John Black	(JB)	Vernon Janke	(VJ)
Clement Brigl	(CB)	Orville Jones	(OJ)
Robert Christie	(RC)	Clifford Knapp	(CK)
George Donaldson	(GD)	Jack Metcalfe	(JM)
Robert Facklam	(RF)	Bora Simmons	(BS)
John Gneckow	(JG)	William Stark	(WS)
Oswald Goering	(OG)	Bessel VandenHazel	(BV)
Pat Guilday	(PG)	Robert Vogl	(RV)
Donald Hammerman	(DH)	Sonia Vogl	(SV)

Illustrations by Pat Guilday, Betsi McKay, & Jane Klep

Malcolm D. Swan

Table of Contents

XV. Weather

XVI. Winter Studies

XVII. Environmental Values

I. Conducting Field Experiences

It has long been recognized that our continued welfare rests upon the wise use of natural resources. Students begin to grasp this large concept as they explore, investigate, understand, and enjoy the environment in which they live and play. Field trips, both near and far, should place students in settings and situations which prompt their asking questions, making observations, measuring, collecting data, interviewing, discussing, reviewing, and interpreting. A spirit of curiosity and exploration on the part of both the leader and the students is a most essential ingredient for successful study in the field.

This chapter consists of six sections that may assist teachers or leaders as they plan and conduct outdoor experiences. They contain tips on:

1. The reasons for providing outdoor or field experiences.

2. Teacher preparation.

3. Preparing the learners.

4. Conducting the experience.

5. Follow-up.

6. Questions that leaders should ask while preparing to use nature's classroom.

Why Provide Outdoor or Field Experiences?

Learning horizons extend beyond the classroom, across town, and far into the country. As we knock on the surface of the moon, it is not enough for our children to remain in classrooms and look out. They must experience directly the excitement, pressures, and problems of the real world.

To help make instruction real, teachers and leaders often provide sensory experiences and field excursions away from the classroom. These are important reasons for utilizing real outdoor environments as an extension of the school curriculum:

1. To arouse curiosity and prepare for a new unit of study.

2. To stimulate added interest in a given area or unit of study. (Students now will have some background and can ask more penetrating questions.)

3. To culminate a unit of study. (Specific activities on the field trip may clarify unclear ideas and even rekindle interest.)

4. To collect or obtain specimens to bring back to the classroom for additional study. (Plants, insects, soils, rocks, etc., may often be studied best on "location," but some phases lend themselves to classroom or laboratory study.)

5. To observe and record data. (Differences in the stages of animal and plant growth, a person's location at a historic time, or the environmental impact of constructing a manufacturing plant must be studied in the field.)

6. To illustrate the sociological relationships in out-of-school activities. (To learn about the world of work.)

7. To gain an esthetic appreciation of a historic event by studying the site where it occurred (town meeting place, courtroom, state capitol building, battlefield, launching pad, etc.).

8. To improve student use of leisure time.

9. To help students better understand our planet and all that it contains. (Small bits and pieces become integral parts of a total picture as one's horizons are broadened.)

Preparation by the Teacher

Much study and preplanning must go into every field trip. Tips for planning range from the usual safety precautions through parent and student involvement:

1. Make a "dry-run" or personal visit to the site prior to making the actual trip with the class. There is no better way than this to avoid potential problems.

2. Meet with the host or guide and explain the purposes of the visit, students' ages, the kinds of questions that are likely to be asked, the time available, and the material to be covered. What will the children do in preparation and follow-up?

3. Check material needs for the trip such as special apparatus, clothing for the students, food, drink, and expense money. (Rest or comfort stops are needed for long trips, especially for younger children.)

4. Plan travel activities for the students both to and from the field-trip site. (This may include observing, recording information, keeping a time log, etc.)

5. Secure approvals from the school authorities, the owners of the site you will visit, and the parents of the children. All should be informed about the purposes of the trip; where, when, and how you will travel; the costs that will be encountered; and how these expenses will be handled.

6. Plan for adequate supervision, and consult with the school principal or your supervisor concerning your plans. Parents and other interested persons may be able to accompany the group. A ratio of one adult per 8 or 10 children is usually recommended. Provide adults with a list of the children for whom they are responsible. A briefing session prior to the day of the trip helps to establish guidelines as to what is expected. Some principals and directors are excellent helpers on a field trip.

7. Make follow-up plans before you conduct the field trip. Follow-up experiences are extremely important. When these call for a sharing and reviewing of the experiences on the field trip, they create a lasting impression.

Preparing the Children for the Trip

Children are keenly interested in field trips away from the school; hence, the carry-over may be great if careful planning takes place. We offer these suggestions:

1. Help the children to understand the reasons for the trip. (Children need to have some basic understanding of the problem at hand and some general background knowledge in order to understand how this out-of-school experience relates to their total school program.)

2. Prepare the children to observe carefully, make accurate recordings, and make critical reviews and appraisals. (Prior practice along these lines is needed. One cannot teach these skills in a few minutes, and the field trip itself is neither the time nor the place to introduce them.)

3. Give the students the purpose they need for learning. Explain that a field trip can provide them with opportunities to apply their classroom learning.

4. Beforehand, help the children feel that the field trip will be an interesting and worthwhile experience, not just another lesson or set of facts. Let your enthusiasm show!

5. Assign a specific responsibility or job to each and every member of the class so that each one is involved in the project. (Appoint recorders, observers, guides, feelers, smellers, etc.)

6. Communicate your expectations about behavior and conduct. When this is fully discussed, the children will better understand what is expected of them and realize why rules must be followed. Children can help establish the rules and list many cautions to be observed when visiting the field-trip site.

7. Use the buddy system or a small-team approach to help to keep track of the children. Work this out before leaving the school, and let the children in on it. When there are children of various ages on the same trip, appoint older students to act as aides or guides for younger students.

While on the Outdoor Experience

Although outdoor or field experiences are provided for purposes jointly shared by the adults and children, each person will also have his or her own private objectives to meet. On the field trip, the teacher or leader serves mainly as a guide in helping the learners with their observing, recording, and analyzing. Since nothing ruins a field trip more than a lack of enthusiasm on the part of the leader, SHOW ENTHUSIASM.

1. Make sure that the group arrives and departs on time—especially if other groups are also using the site.

2. Do not rush the children into an activity at the site until they become oriented to their new surroundings. (The apprehension of a new place may overshadow any benefits, so take time to see that the participants are comfortable and know their starting and ending places.)

3. Use public transportation when possible. (The professionals know routes, travel times, and things to see or to avoid and can concentrate on the driving.) This leaves you free to work with the learners and aides.

4. Plan for comfort or rest stops prior to the trip on short hauls and upon arrival after long trips to help to improve participants' attitudes and behavioral patterns. (Avoid taking or purchasing food unless the trip covers the lunch period.)

5. Allow sufficient time for observations and data gathering, but keep the action lively and varied. The capacity for sustained interest varies, and the pace must take interest spans into consideration.

6. Impress upon the students that their behavior reflects on the total school and that their behavior, good or bad, will determine if subsequent groups will be welcome at the site.

7. Take a head count at each stop and always know where every child is. In large groups, color coding helps participants to recognize their group. (Name tags with school, address, and telephone number are a must for young children.)

8. Always follow common basic rules of courtesy, and observe the basic rules of safety. Warn students of the hazards at the site.

Afterwards: Evaluation and Follow-up

Follow-up may be the most important phase of the field trip. If the leader shows no interest in what the children have done or fails to encourage them to express their reactions, he or she is indirectly telling them that the entire thing was of no importance. Evaluating the experience with learners helps to determine if the specific visitation should be undertaken at another time with another group.

1. Build upon the field experience, and encourage the learners to seek answers to the problems they encountered.

2. Inform parents about the experience. (Written exercises describing the events and activities help to convey ideas to the parents and to the public at large.)

3. Recognize that the social experience of being with persons other than the family and the actual ride on the bus may be important aspects of the trip. (Children and adults tend to work better and to learn more readily when they enjoy their work and are with other people.)

4. Relate personal observations and investigations to the classroom activities individually through reports, projects, demonstrations, displays, and group presentations. (A list of things learned by youngsters is not enough; tie the ideas to the on-going school program.)

5. List ideas or questions that were raised or unanswered on the trip to determine if additional excursions or study are needed. Gathered data should be analyzed and hypotheses evaluated in terms of the problems under study.

6. File a written evaluation for future reference. This evaluation could be jointly developed with the help of the children and can be of value to others when they plan a similar trip.

7. Factual information as to sites used, routes, and persons to contact should be made a part of the permanent record. Eventually, this will lead to a *Field Trip Resource Guide* at the school or camp.

A Planning Guide to the Outdoor Experience

Whatever its purposes, the outdoor activity should be preceded and followed by thinking, planning, and evaluation. Teachers and leaders need to think about questions like these before they take a group of youngsters outdoors:

Self-preparation:

1. What do you know about the children's attention spans, previous experiences, need for controls, skills in the language arts, etc.?

2. What do you know about mechanical concerns such as (1) transportation, (2) snacks, (3) permission to go to the site and to use facilities, (4) clothing and equipment, (5) people to contact, (6) water and toilet facilities available, (7) routes to take, and (8) length of trip?

3. What do you need to know regarding the skills and content areas?

4. What concepts and understandings will you try to develop? What do you hope to accomplish?

Preparation of the children:

1. How will you introduce the experience?

2. What things are the children to plan, and what will you plan? Do the children understand their role in planning?

3. What knowledge do the children bring to the situation, and what is lacking?

4. What are the children to learn? As a group? As individuals?

5. How will they record their experience (individual efforts, group recorders, picture taking, or various combinations)?

6. Who will develop behavior standards? What will they be? Are there "musts" from the point-of-view of health and safety?

7. What other forms of the language arts can be woven into the experience (interviewing, introductions, listening with a purpose)?

During the experience:

1. How can you ensure that the children derive the greatest value from the experience?

2. How much talking and telling by you is really necessary?

3. What leading questions can you ask that will actively involve the children in looking, listening, and trying to explain?

4. Are you trying to cover too much? Are too many concepts involved?

5. Are too many skills being demanded of the children?

6. Are the questions posed before the trip being answered?

7. Are the relationships between things evident? Are the children seeing them?

8. Are the children showing signs that they need a change of pace?

Evaluating the experience with children:

1. What did we do? What did we learn?

2. What were the big ideas (generalizations)?

3. What did we like about the trip? What didn't we like?

4. Were our behavior standards sufficient? Did we meet them?

5. What new questions have arisen?

6. How can we make our experience a permanent one? How can we share it with others?

Follow-up activities:

1. What can the children talk about and write about? In what ways can we use poetry, drama, imaginative stories, and factual accounts to convey what we learned to others?

2. What pictorial representations of the experience can be developed?

3. What symbolic interpretations can we make of the trip? How will we explain the symbolism to others so they can understand it?

4. How will we communicate what we learned to parents? What will we communicate?

II. Animal Studies

Nearly all children are interested in animals; hence, little motivation is needed when it comes to the study of birds, insects, mammals, and the like. Furthermore, interest and enthusiasm in this regard can often be utilized by teachers and leaders to induce children to read, write, observe, and gather data.

This section consists of several guides, informational sheets, and teaching tips that have been helpful to teachers when initiating and conducting various kinds of animal studies.

Animal Tracking

Animals, unlike plants, tend to move from one place to another, and this makes their study entirely different. Special methods for collecting, counting, and studying them are needed, and different methods may be used for studying a species at different stages of its life. The variety of life in the animal kingdom is astonishing. Some animals live on the ground, some in it, others live in the sea, some use the air, and many share our homes.

An aspect of an outdoor-animal study that promotes group interest and involvement is that of reading animal tracks and preserving them by using plaster. The following are tips for working with children on experiences of this nature.

Reading the Tracks

Discuss with the group the kinds of animals likely to be found in the particular location. A review of the specific food and shelter needs of the individual animals should bring out the specific areas to investigate for tracks. Generally, more tracks will be found in a location that has damp, soft, or pliable surfaces, such as a cultivated field, stream bank, sandy beach, or base of a tree. Upon discovering tracks, trackers should be careful so that none are damaged until the study has been completed. Information about the tracks can be obtained by measuring dimensions and determining type of foot, such as hoofed, toed, clawed, or padded.

Distances between, direction taken, and depth of tracks are other clues to be considered. Questions like the following may be used for group discussion to help stimulate interest and curiosity.

Single Tracks:

> How long is the track?
> How wide is the track?
> How many toes on a forefoot?
> How many toes on a hindfoot?
> Is the track fresh or old?

Group Tracks:

> What direction was the animal traveling?
> Was the animal walking or running?
> Does the animal continue at the same speed?
> What other signs of the animal are present?
> What are the feet adapted for (climbing, grasping, running)?
> What kind of food might this animal eat?

After the group has made a thorough investigation of the tracks, individuals should have an opportunity to take home a souvenir track.

WHO GOES THERE?

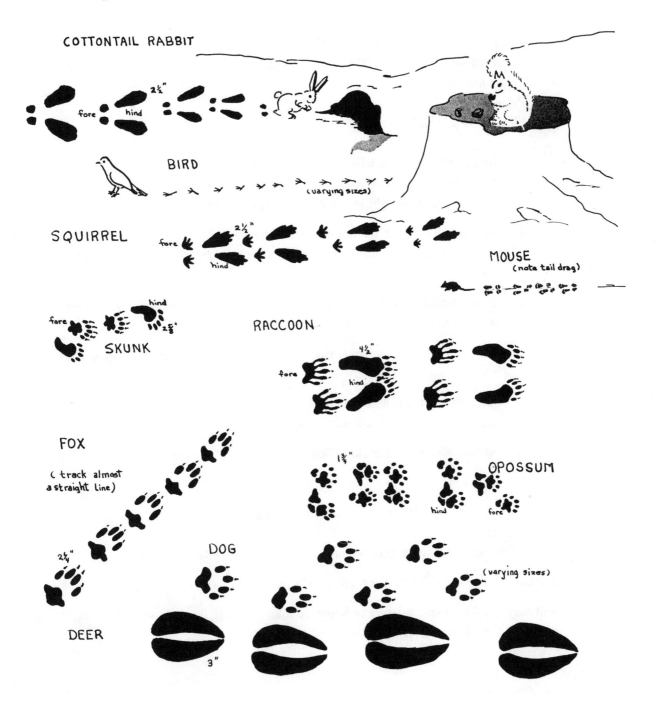

COTTONTAIL RABBIT

fore   hind   2½"

BIRD
(varying sizes)

SQUIRREL
fore   2½"
hind

MOUSE
(note tail drag)

SKUNK
fore   hind   2⅝"

RACCOON
fore   4½"
hind

FOX
(track almost
a straight line)
2¼"

1¾"   OPOSSUM
hind   fore

DOG
(varying sizes)

DEER
3"

Preserving Tracks (Plaster Casting)

Several methods are available for preserving tracks for later follow-up study and include sketching, photographing, and replica casting. The following technique has worked well for making plaster casts of tracks.

Equipment: (for group of 8 or 10)
Three cans (#10 size) with plastic lids.
Construction paper or file folders cut into strips about 4 centimeters (1.5 inches) wide (for making collars).
Paper clips.
Plaster of Paris and water.

Procedure:

1. Select the track you will "cast" and remove any loose materials that might have fallen into it. Position a strip of the construction paper around it to form a collar, making sure it is tight to the ground so plaster will not seep out.

2. Mix enough plaster for the number of tracks to be cast. Pour some plaster into one of the cans, add water, and stir until the mixture is the consistency of pancake batter.

3. Pour carefully into the track to be cast. Some forms of plaster begin to set within a few minutes, so do not dawdle.

4. Before the plaster hardens, shape a paper clip to serve as a hanging hook, and secure it into the plaster.

5. After the plaster is hardened (one-half to three hours), carefully remove the collar. Gently clean off the cast with an old brush.

6. Mount the cast to a backing board to make an attractive decoration.

Other Possibilities or Tips

1. Casts of leaves and flowers may be painted with poster paints or oil paints.

2. Talcum powder sprinkled on the track will keep the cast from retaining sand or mud.

3. Salt may be added to the mixture to hasten setting. Vinegar slows down the setting. Dental plaster, although expensive, sets very quickly.

Animal Homes

The following was prepared to introduce the idea of involving children in the study of "animal homes." It is not an attempt to cover the subject, there being a variety of materials available that provide detailed descriptions on this subject.

Promoting Involvement—Group Planning

Before departing for the field, the group should decide on several simple objectives, and the activities to undertake. The type of activity planned determines what equipment will be needed.

Thought should also be given to what might be the most logical places in which to find the types of homes being sought. Factors such as food and water sources and the need for protection should be considered when planning the route. The children should be aware that animals prefer southern-slope areas in cold weather and that the north, sunless slopes are the poorest and the least likely to be inhabited.

Activities for Studying Animal Homes

1. Determine location and number of entrances to the home. Discuss possible reasons for using the particular location.

2. Measure and compare size of holes, size of nests, etc., and the distances between the different entrances when more than one are present.

3. Gather and analyze food scraps (bones, feathers) discarded outside.

4. Determine the differences between outside air temperature and the temperature within the entrance.

5. Determine if the home is in use (lay small pieces of materials—grass, fine sand, etc.—around the entrance if in doubt).

6. Discuss whether the animal's living habits change during the year.

7. Make plaster casts of tracks around the home, if available.

8. Set a trap to capture the animal alive. Seek further instructions on suggestions for this activity.

More Items for Discussion

1. Did the animal that lives here build the home?

2. Is the home located so the animal can observe without being seen?

3. Is the home located for warmth?

4. What habits of the owner are revealed by what is found here?

5. What are likely to be the enemies of this animal?

Helpful References

Jaeger, Ellsworth, *Tracks and Trailcraft,* The Macmillan Company, New York, 1948.

Mason, George F., *Animal Homes,* William Morrow & Co., Inc., New York, 1947.

Murie, Alous J., *A Field Guide to Animal Tracks,* Second Edition, Houghton Mifflin Company, Boston, 1975.

Insect Signs

Insect signs are often more apparent than the insects themselves, even in warm weather. Insect homes such as galls, leafminer tunnels, leaf-roller cases, cocoons, mud nests, and tunnels in wood and earth are clues to the presence of insects.

Galls. Galls are abnormal swellings or growths found on almost any part of a plant. Galls may be caused by bacteria, viruses, mites, flies, and bees. The mechanism causing them is relatively obscure, but rapid, uncontrolled cell division appears to occur in the plant tissue in response to foreign material within it. In the case of insect galls, the female insect inserts one or more eggs into the plant tissue, triggering the response.

Galls may be collected and dried after placement in a killing jar. However, it is interesting to try to rear the insects. The entire plant can be potted and brought indoors, or the study can go on outdoors. In any event, the simplest way to collect the adult insect is to construct a fine net cage around the gall until it emerges. Some gall insects have parasites that lay their eggs inside the gall. Their young feed on the developing gall insect.

Leafminers. Leafminers are insects that develop within a leaf. An egg is inserted between the upper and lower layers of leaf tissue. The young insect eats the spongy tissues, thus producing irregular blotches or tunnels. A careful observer can learn a great deal about the developing insect since the living, wormlike insect can often be seen when the leaf is held up to the light. These insects can be reared in the same manner as gall insects, but since some pupate in the soil, the entire plant may need to be caged. There are about 500 species of miners in the United States, and each has a characteristic "mine" in a particular plant.

Leaf-rollers. Leaf-rollers are insects that roll leaves into "homes." Some use a cluster of leaves or individual leaves, but most cut portions of a leaf and roll them. Once you have recognized this group, you find they are more common than one might suspect. Most leaf-rollers are moths or butterflies, and most use the leaves of only one kind of plant.

Paper Nests. The paper nest of the bald-faced hornet *(Vespula* maculata) is quite distinctive. This insect chews wood into a gray, paper-like material and constructs a nest, often larger than a football, somewhat globular, and usually attached to a tree or shrub. The hornet itself is large, black, and light yellow with the front of the head light yellow (bald-faced). Caution: This insect has one of the most potent stings found in the insect world.

Other wasps make paper nests, but these are generally tan in color, smaller, and less elaborate than those of the bald-faced hornet. If the nest is occupied, stay away and do not annoy or upset these insects. They will sting repeatedly if upset.

Mud Nests. Mud nests are made by some wasps. The nest of the "organpipe" wasp can be found on buildings or rock outcroppings. These nests are tubes up to about 20 centimeters (8 inches) long placed alongside of each other. The adults use these tubes as "nurseries" rather than as homes. The tubes are chambered, each chamber containing an egg with enough paralyzed insects to provide food for the developing larva.

Potter wasps form small jug- or vase-shaped mud nests on tree branches. Each "pot" contains an egg with food.

Ground Nests. Yellow-jackets, bumble bees, and some of their relatives dig burrows into the ground. Yellow-jacket nests, for instance, contain many individuals.

Most people are familiar with ant nests. Many ants live in the ground, but carpenter ants tunnel extensively into dead or diseased wood. The nests of carpenter ants are not easily confused with those of termites because, in general, termites leave no apparent outward signs except for a paper-thin shell of wood. Termites work very fast, and their nests must somehow remain in contact with the soil; hence, pencil-thick tunnels of mud are often constructed for long distances by termites between nest and soil.

Bark Tunnels. Often, when bark is stripped from logs, the tunnels made by bark beetles between the bark and the wood become apparent. The most fascinating of these tunnels consists of a long, usually vertical channel in which the female lays the eggs. Radiating out from the eggs are twisty channels gradually increasing in width that were made by the larvae as they developed. Large-scale infestations of these beetles can girdle and kill a tree.

Insects for Winter Study

Since insects are coldblooded and least active in cold weather, specimens can be difficult to find in the winter. Adult insects of many sorts hibernate under logs and rocks, in weed clumps, grass tufts, crevices, and among fallen litter. In the coldest weather it is possible to find fairly active insects among the downy leaves of mullein plants. Occasionally, a hatch occurs in the winter, and thousands of "springtails" may be seen on the snow.

One way to obtain insects almost any time is to place a mass of forest-floor litter into a separator of some sort. One form of a separator is a modified Berlese funnel (see illustration). To construct this device, use a funnel with a screen of about 6-millimeter (¼-inch) mesh part way down to hold the litter. Next, place a light (hopefully with an inverted funnel-shaped reflector) above it. As the litter dries and heats, insects work their way down the spout away from the light and heat of the bulb. Place a small jar under the funnel to catch them.

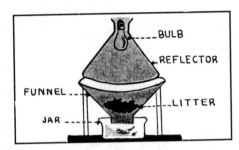

Soil insects. If a section of hard-frozen earth is taken indoors and warmed, a number of insects may emerge. Soil from areas covered by water in the spring often contains large numbers of mosquito eggs. They can be hatched by placing the soil in a dish of water for a day or two. Other forms of life may also appear when this is done, so expect to be surprised.

Fallen logs harbor many sorts and stages of insects in winter. Some will be between the wood and the bark, while others (beetles, ants, wasps, and bees) will be in the wood itself. Examining them outdoors is a good way to study many insects with powerful venom in comparative safety as they are quite sluggish when cold. The ants, bees, and wasps found in these places are often fertilized queens capable of producing new colonies.

Rock cracks harbor many insects, especially beetles hibernating for the winter. On sunny winter days many dormant insects revive a bit and fly or crawl about. The south-facing sides of rock outcroppings and stone buildings are the most likely spots.

Insects can also be found in buildings throughout the year. High-shelter areas are the best places to look. It is likely that the flies taking shelter in buildings during the winter produce most of the young that plague us in the summer. For insects that are parasites of warm-blooded animals, life is often "as usual" throughout the winter.

Making an Insect Collection

Collecting:

Materials Needed:

A butterfly net.

Killing jar—a jar and lid with cotton or plaster in the bottom.

Killing chemical—a variety of chemicals are used. They can be purchased from science supply houses.

Collection jars—small jars with lids (baby food jars).

Notebook.

Pencil.

Identification books.

Making a Net:

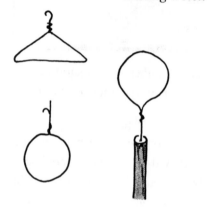

Shape a heavy wire (coat hanger) to form a ring of 25 to 30 centimeters (10 to 12 inches) in diameter with ends extending 8 to 10 centimeters (3 to 4 inches) to tie as a handle. The bag should be made from a material such as bobbinet or Bruzelle cloth and tapered to about 10 centimeters (4 inches) as the diameter at the end. It should be about three times as long as the diameter of the wire ring and attached firmly to it.

Catching Insects:

Look around and under rocks, bark, logs, grass, etc., for insects. Catch those you can by hand and place in the jars. Record the date and location.

To catch a flying insect, move the net slowly toward it until within 25 to 30 centimeters (10 to 12 inches) of it. Quickly move the net over the insect, and flip it over the ring to trap the insect. Insert the killing jar (with lid removed) into the net, and trap the insect in the jar with the net serving as a lid. As you remove the jar from the net, slip the lid onto it.

18

The Killing Jar: Saturate the cotton plaster in the bottom of the killing jar with the killing chemical, and put the lid on tight. When you have an insect in your net, transfer it to the killing jar. When the insect is dead, remove it and place it in another jar.

Drying:

Materials Needed: Insect pins.
Pinning board.
Cardboard.

The Pinning Board: The pinning board notch should be narrower at one end, and sides should be sloped slightly upwards (see illustration).

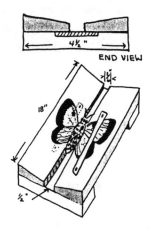

Use the pinning board to dry insects with spread wings, such as moths, butterflies, dragon flies, and damsel flies and to dry the left wing of grasshoppers. Run the pin through the thorax and slightly to the right of the midline. Place the body in the groove and pin the wings down. The body should be straight up and down on the pin. Wasps and other long, thin insects may be pinned through the side of the thorax.

Mounting:

Materials Needed: Mounting boxes (cigar boxes or something similar) with the bottoms lined with corrugated cardboard (or similar soft material).
Insect pins.
Labels for identification.

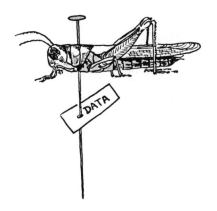

Directions: Consult keys and references for assistance in classifying and naming your specimens. Make a label for each containing the name of the specimen, date and location of its capture, and collector's name.

Position the insect about 0.5 centimeter (0.25 inch) below the pinhead, place the label about a centimeter (inch) below the insect, and position the pin into the bottom of the box so that it is straight up and down.

Arrange the collection artistically by families and subfamilies. A mothball pinned inside the box helps to preserve the collection.

Animals in the Classroom

At a time when humans are striving for environmental awareness at all ages and levels, living things in the classroom may help speed the development of the "web of life" concept. Plants or animals in the classroom are an endless source of enjoyment, curiosity, wonderment, and knowledge. They can provide valuable learning experiences in observation, data recording, experimentation, problem-solving, reading, interviewing, and discussing. Observing the processes of growth and reproduction and being responsible for the special care and handling of the different plants and animals offers a valuable learning experience.

Animals adaptable to a classroom environment may vary from community to community, so be sure to check for specific rules of your own school district or city. In general, the types of animals chosen for the classroom should be selected for the ages of the children involved, the concepts to be developed, the care required, and the safety precautions to be considered. Mammals such as rabbits, mice, white rats, hamsters, and guinea pigs predominate. Aquariums of fish are often found in the classroom. Snakes, frogs, and birds are less often present.

Questions for investigation include the following:

1. What foods are recommended for a specific animal?

2. How much and how often should food be given?

3. What patterns can be studied relative to growth, housing, exercise, and socialization?

Some cautions and concerns for student discussion and investigation include the following:

1. Specific plans for daily care such as cleaning, feeding, and watering. Perhaps a schedule of students to be responsible for these chores could be established.

2. Care of animal over weekends and holidays. (This may become a real problem.)

3. Requirements for housing such as a cage or a darkened living area; an exercise area; and freedom from excess noise, heat, drafts, lights, and other environmental factors.

4. Storage of food and medicines, disposal of litter and refuse from cages, and disinfection of equipment.

5. Reaction to the odors.

6. Provisions for the care of the animal when school ends for the year or during vacations.

Responsibility, kindness, and concern for life requirements accompanying the care of living things may help to enhance the student's feeling of worth and responsibility, even though this may not be the main reason for having the animals in the classroom. The first-hand direct experience with animals in the classroom may meet a very important need of some youngsters and may lead to much more than expected.

Observation of Animals in a Museum or Zoo

Just as the classroom rearing of living things enhances learning, so too will the study of animals in a museum or zoo. Human links with the past and a way of life far different from that of the student in today's classroom may be relived through a visit to a museum or zoo.

The Museum: 1. What animals were once common in your home area?

2. Do they have any present-day relatives there?

3. Which of these are on the endangered species list?

4. What were the geographic distributions of those animals?

5. What were their major sources of food?

6. What were their habitat needs?

7. What is the present status of these animals—and these habitats?

The Zoo: Animals in a zoo are more likely representative of widely differing geographic locations and situations. As such, they allow for questions and studies such as the following:

1. What can we learn about the numbers of this species of animal and its distribution?

2. Which of its relatives are wild in our own area?

3. What are the food requirements of this animal?

4. What are its habitat requirements?

5. Is this animal kept alone—or are a number of individuals housed together? Does it "mix" with other species?

Make observations such as the following:

1. Record any sounds, actions, and characteristics you observe. (Through additional study, determine the advantage of such characteristics and behaviors.)

2. Record information about the physical arrangement of the zoo. Does the placement of animals, physical barriers, and the like tend to simulate real-life situations?

3. Develop conclusions concerning health and safety for humans and beasts. Are the specialized needs of each animal being met?

A study of humans and their interactions with the caged animals may reveal some characteristics that indicate why some animals may be on endangered species lists and why certain animals have been portrayed in song and story. As with any other field activity, preplanning for safety and comfort as well as the educational value are of utmost importance to a successful visit to a museum or zoo.

Birds and Binoculars

Although you are likely to see many more different kinds of birds than mammals on an outing, the birds are more difficult to identify. From a distance, a vulture may be mistaken for an eagle, and the color patterns of warblers may escape the untrained eye as the birds move along so quickly. With hundreds of species, including those which pass through twice a year in migration, and many of which are similar in habit and coloration, you must develop an alert eye to be able to identify the birds that flash across your view.

1. Observations should begin in your own backyard. A birdfeeder is a good place to observe birds, but be sure to have a good "bird book" or guide on hand for quick reference. And, if you begin the winter season with a birdfeeder, be sure that feed is made available *every* day throughout the winter.

2. An item of equipment almost essential to bird study is a pair of binoculars. They are an extension of one's vision, and you should purchase the best that you can afford. Those of the 7×35 variety give adequate enlargement for most purposes and are still light enough so that they are not cumbersome for extended use in the field. Spend some time practicing with your binoculars so that you become very proficient in quickly getting them to your eyes and adjusting them. Many birds don't stop more than a few seconds before moving to another perch.

3. A very appropriate activity for children and teachers is to keep a "life list" of birds seen. As you see a new bird, record information about it (date, where seen, etc.). By keeping such a record you know where you stand as a birder.

4. Another approach is the keeping of a "class list" of birds. As each species is seen and identified for the first time in the year by a class member, record the date, location, name of observer, and means of verification on a wall chart.

Recognize that no one has ever become a competent ornithologist or birder in a week or a month. However, a few trips taken with individuals "who know their birds" and a little practice will give you the beginning of a lifelong hobby. Some birders travel hundreds, even thousands, of miles to add one new "lifer." And, as a teacher, recognize that only a few of the kinds of the birds in an area will appear on the schoolgrounds or at the feeder. Each bird has its own specific habitat, and several class field trips to the various habitats may be appropriate to "complete" the class list.

Using a Clue Chart for Bird Identification

The clue chart is very useful when recording information about a bird seen at the feeder or in the wild. Record information about the bird in the appropriate space of the clue chart. The information may be in the form of words, sketches, or whatever is most meaningful in describing the bird and its behavior.

	Size	Shade	Shape	Surroundings	Sweep	Song
1.						
2.						
3.						

Some Characteristics

Size: Is the bird larger than a sparrow (15 cm/6 in.)? A robin (24 cm/10 in.)? A crow (50 cm/20 in.)?

Shade: Areas of the body where colors are located (variations in color at the throat, belly, wings, and tail and markings of feathers).

Shape: Body – (plump, sleek, thin, short and stubby, streamlined).
      Bill – (thick, thin, long, short).
      Tail – (rounded, wedged, squared, notched).
      Wing – (rounded, pointed, ragged).
      Leg – (long, short).

Surroundings: Where was the bird located (tree top, vertical position on tree trunk, wooded area, meadow, telephone wire, fence post, prairie, along a country road, swimming or floating on water, other)?

Sweep: What were the flight characteristics (jerky, darting, swooping, irregular)?

Song: Are there phonetic sounds (raspy, chip-chip, peter-peter, trill)?

III. Awareness and Creative Expression

One reason for working outdoors with children is to develop "awareness of surroundings," a first step in developing a concern for environmental conditions and what some refer to as "environmental conscience."

Furthermore, such experiences provide the material, setting, and inspiration for creative language arts activities.

This section consists of several tips and suggestions that teachers have found to be helpful.

Awareness of the World Around Us

Awareness experiences may take many forms. *Listen* to the sounds around you, and record them on tape to demonstrate how we "shut out" noises. *Smell* the bricks, soil, bark of trees, etc. *Taste* (using discretion) some of the plants common to the area. *Look* for different shapes, colors, and designs, and compare the human-made structured shapes with natural shapes. *Look* for regular and irregular patterns. *Touch* and *feel* the bark of trees, the soil, the texture of leaves. Using the senses in these ways helps children to become aware of what is around them.

Assist learners in utilizing the information they obtain through these experiences and to place it into perspective. The synthesis of observational information requires different skills than merely learning names and answering specific questions about that which is being examined.

Much can be learned about the various forms of life by examining specimens closely and noting where they are found. Notice the color, shape, and size of an animal. Take a closer look at its outer covering (scales, fur, feathers, or spines). Look for the size and placement of eyes and mouth.

Notice the shape of the beak of a bird. Is it short and heavy (a seed eater) or light and slender (an insect eater)? Does the bird have long legs and a long bill (shore birds)? Does it fly steadily, or does it flutter and glide like the woodpecker?

Change continually occurs in all forms of life. By observing a living thing at periodic intervals over several days or weeks, important insights can be gained. Spend several minutes each day examining a particular leaf or bud system on a plant.

The broader spectrum of observational activities may also be applied to observing community traffic patterns, businesses, and industries. The important factor, however, *is to go to that which is being studied and study it in its own environment.*

Tips for Observing and Studying in the Outdoors

One goal of outdoor teaching activities is to provide for first-hand observation of various phenomena which leads to distinguishing the unique characteristics of the focus of the experience. If this is to be achieved, children must be taught how to observe, how to determine what is important, and how to organize the data they gather for use.

You may learn much about your students by noting the responses they give during an unstructured observational activity. Notice the vocabulary they use to describe items. Is there good use of descriptive terms? Are pertinent observations made? Is a mental picture of the phenomenon transmitted? What techniques are used for recording (writing, pictures, or some other symbols)? Is time of observation or location noted? What senses are used?

A beginning activity might be to examine a tree. Have each student select a tree, make many types of observations, and record these observations in writing. After 15 to 20 minutes ask the students to read their descriptions. As they read, can others in the group identify the tree being described? Will a sketch really help to clarify any points?

Have the students select the items that seem most important and organize them in sequence on a card. For trees, include items such as leaves, shape of tree, bark description, location, size, branching, smell of crushed leaf, taste of twig, etc. These could then be compared with clues given in tree finders or other tree reference books used for identification.

Procedures like these may also be used with rocks, herbs, mammals, birds, and insects. Clue cards or clue charts can also be used to record data about any form of life. Unstructured initial experiences can help students to understand that they can collect data about many things, even though they know little about the object being examined. Such investigative approaches have important implications for eventual development of scientific techniques.

Awareness of the Environment

Discovering more and more about one's own environment can be an exciting venture. We do not become aware of the objects found in our immediate surroundings merely because we have sense organs. Many look but do not see. They become aware of their surroundings only to the degree they are afforded opportunities for careful observation.

These activities may help to sharpen students' senses:

1. Discover objects relating to *texture* which can be described as slick, hard, rough, soft, slimy, velvety, coarse, knobby, ribbed, furry, hairy, waxy, spongy, lumpy, etc.

2. Discover objects relating to *shape* which can be described as oval, round, oblong, lobed, ridged, smooth-edged, rough-edged, triangular, pointed, curved, etc.

3. Discover objects relating to *density* which can be described as solid, thick, hollow, compact, porous, non-porous, heavy, light, etc.

4. Discover objects relating to *temperature* which can be described as hot, cold, damp, clammy, moist, dry, wet, cool, lukewarm, etc.

5. Discover objects relating to *size* which can be described as narrow, large, small, tall, short, thick, heavy, bulky, miniature, etc.

6. Look for evidence of life "above and around water" including insects, turtles, algae and other plants, worms, frogs, etc.

7. Observe the differences in the "bark of trees." Some bark may be shaggy, some may resemble potato chips, some may adopt the shapes and colors found on the back of certain snakes, some may have warty-like projections, and some may have deep ridges.

8. Look for "domestic" and "wild" flowers. Examine them carefully to note the number, color, size, and shape of the petals.

9. Measure out an area of about 1,000 square centimeters (or about 1 square foot) of ground using a piece of string. Categorize the various forms of plant and animal life found in this area. Also, classify according to "kind" the other types of organic materials found there.

A 1,000-Square-Centimeter (1-Square-Foot) Field Trip

Directions: Have students work individually or in pairs. Instruct them to "explore and tally" those items which they find in 1,000 square centimeters (1 square foot) or some other small area of ground.

Have the students categorize and classify all items found, whether human-made or natural. Names or descriptions may be used.

Have them look specifically for the following types of "evidence" and record their findings.

1. Name the materials or objects found in your area, and, if possible, tally the frequency with which each appears.

2. Is there evidence that some materials have undergone change? Describe some of the changes.

3. Is there evidence of the presence of "humans" in the area? Explain the kind of evidence.

4. Which objects or phenomena lend themselves to further investigation?

5. Arrange the names of the objects found into some given sequence or order.

6. Using the names of the objects, determine common characteristics of each and organize these into a key or guide to help identify the object—such as a dichotomous (either/or) key.

7. Try to find objects in your area whose names begin with every letter of the alphabet.

8. After being given a list of things to look for and working in teams (each on a particular plot), see which team can find the largest number or percentage of items on the list.

Creative Expression

The outdoors provides a setting many people find comforting and relaxing. Here it seems natural to relax and to think and feel differently than when occupied in the routine of ordinary daily life. One can reflect on topics such as "the meaning of life" or "truth" or "peace in the countryside" or whatever. The outdoors provides a setting that encourages expressions in prose and poetry.

Some people like to express their thoughts orally; others like to express them in writing. By reading appropriate poetry or narratives, children will begin to "express themselves" and become more aware of their surroundings. Set the stage and let each individual go alone to a quiet spot to "think his or her own thoughts" and to "feel his or her own feelings." Encourage each one to record, in writing, reflections about whatever comes to mind.

If poetry is being stressed, one thought should be emphasized. For beginners, short phrases or narratives emphasizing feelings or expanding on experiences provide a starting point. Many children enjoy writing Haiku and Cinquain poetry.

Haiku poetry consists of three lines of five, seven, and five syllables. The emphasis is on syllabic form not rhyme. The art of Haiku is to capture in words the "quick reaction" one gets when observing something that dramatically catches the eye. It might be a reaction to a bird in flight, a sunset, an unusual cloud formation, or most anything.

Cinquain (meaning five) poetry also emphasizes syllabic form, but there are five lines. Each line consists of a specific number of syllables and a purpose: (1) states title in two syllables, (2) describes title in four syllables, (3) tells of action in six syllables, (4) expresses a feeling in eight syllables, and (5) uses another word picture for the title in two syllables.

Children may also write stories and songs about their experiences. Lead the children through some unusual experience (outdoor experiences are unusual for some children), and have them write about it. Not only does this help the children to attain new writing heights, but you can also observe the reaction of the children to uncommon experiences and thereby gain an insight of the students' creative expression, which often flows best outside the classroom.

The examples that follow illustrate these types of writing.

1. A poem produced by fifth graders as they sat on a bluff overlooking a stream:

Peaceful Thoughts

As I look at these glistening waters
And see a place where we can drink,
I think to myself what a peaceful world,
But only for a second for then I remember,
I remember the bombs and the fighting
The cars, buses, and the noise
But if only for a second it is still worth the trouble.

2. Thoughts and feelings put into writing while in the forest:

> "For the first time in my life, I felt really close with nature. To feel the winds rustle the trees, the soft sound of birds chirping, the dark, damp, tender soil, life and death in nature—these are the things I've missed all my life, peaceful is the word for this place.

♦ ♦ ♦ ♦ ♦

> "Being with other people, quietly alone gives me the meditative feeling that time means nothing. These are very secure moments of great appreciation. One can almost know the Walden Pond type of peace and contentment. It's marvelous to feel that man has another side from industrialization, urbanization, and materialism."

3. Cinquain: Puppy
               playful, funny
               creeps slowly through the grass
               silently stalks the grasshopper
               hunter

               Camping
               new adventures
               enjoying the outdoors
               freedom from the tensions of school
               joyous

4. Haiku: The star studded tree
            shudders in the moonlight
            The wild wind rushes by

            Dark moving shadow
            passing over the ground
            It is only me.

Tips for Improving Creative Writing

The outdoors provides opportunities for creative writing as well as note taking and other forms of language arts experiences. Good planning is vital, and if children are to write, they should have experiences that provide them with topics for their writing. Below are some "lead up" experiences that may help them to develop positive interests and attitudes about writing:

1. Sensory exploration of natural phenomena:

    a. Have the students close their eyes and touch bark, leaves, feathers, rocks, etc. Have them describe what the objects feel like. Let several persons use descriptive terms to tell what an object feels like to them. Use the other senses in similar ways.

    b. Have the children play games in which attempts are made to describe objects by using similes, metaphors, or comparisons.

    c. Have the children make up short, rhyming descriptions or list as many terms as possible to describe a phenomenon or situation.

2. Use the environment to establish a *mood*. Look out over a vast expanse, look up through the trees to see the patterns of leaves, or examine a hole in the ground or in a tree.

    a. Ask for short, verbal reactions to common and uncommon objects and surroundings.

    b. Select poetry and stories to read that are appropriate for the environment in which you are working (e.g., read poetry about trees and forests when in a wooded area).

    c. Concentrate on a series of short phrases before getting into stories—Haiku poetry is a good introduction to writing for children in the intermediate grades as is writing lyrics to songs about their experiences (to tunes such as "Hey Lolly, Lolly").

    d. Brief, accurate recording of data describing phenomena also has carry-over value into creative writing. Have students focus on smaller, less obvious objects or search for unusual phenomena.

IV. Community Resources

Every community contains elements that can be resources for the educational program. A study of the local community and its history can be exciting if field trips are included to bring children into direct contact and conversation with some of the "old-timers" of the area and into direct contact with the sites and monuments which memorialize important community events.

Such resources are to be found near every school or camp and include farms, parks, monuments, cemeteries, and factories. This section contains examples of materials and learning aids that teachers have used.

No two communities or situations are alike or contain identical resources; hence, teachers or leaders should become thoroughly familiar with the history, economy, and resources of their own local area and develop their own materials to utilize what is available.

Field trips must be well planned if they are to be effective. Students should be involved in the planning process and help in (1) defining the purposes of the trip, (2) determining the process by which data will be gathered, (3) contacting the owners of the property that will be used, (4) developing the code of conduct, and (5) arranging for transportation and meals.

The field trip should be a part of the regular curriculum and not an isolated experience. The information and insights gained through the trip should contribute to the overall objectives of the class and be incorporated into subsequent class activities.

The Cemetery as an Educational Resource

Have you considered the potential educational value of an almost forgotten local cemetery? An examination of the curriculum will reveal possibilities such as these in using such a resource:

1. *Social Studies (local history):*

    Compare dates on headstones as to wars, disease, plague, and early settlement in the area.
    Note burial customs and problems.
    List different nationalities that are represented by the cemetery.

2. *Arithmetic:*

    Calculate the ages of persons at death.
    Find the grave of the oldest person and the oldest grave.
    Inventory the geometric shapes found on the stones.

3. *Science:*

    Investigate the reasons for changes in life span.
    Note types of materials used for gravestones.
    List the effects of time and weathering.
    Discover the occurrences of epidemics.
    Determine cemetery flora and fauna.

4. *Geography:*

    Discuss the design and location of the cemetery.
    Discover the reasons for settling this area or region.

5. *Art:*

    Sketch the designs (decorations) of stones.
    Make transfers and rubbings of gravestones.

Note that the real value of a field trip to a cemetery is achieved only if it is kept directly in the context of on-going studies. Provide time for preplanning with students, and establish some basic educational objectives. Allow time to discuss the rules of respect needed for a cemetery visit.

The following worksheet contains some tips to assist in reaching teaching objectives. About an hour is needed at the cemetery for gathering the information. The final sheet may be completed back in the classroom. Children should be given opportunities during the follow-up to share their experiences.

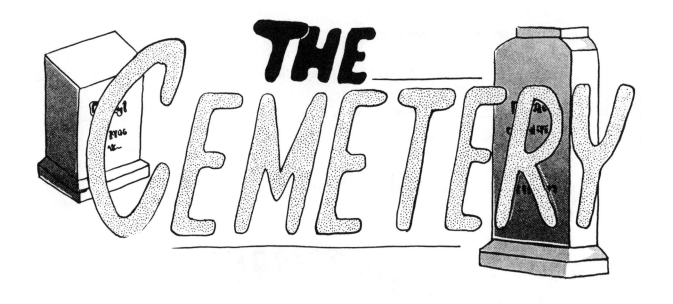

A Journey into the Past

History is learned in many ways. Fossils, artifacts, ruins, and writings help us to learn about our past. Through the study of a cemetery we can learn about how people and life have changed from time to time.

1800's

Full Name	Birth	Death	Age
Zaddock Smith	1830	1877	47
1.			
2.			
3.			
4.			
5.			
6.			
7.			
8.			

1900's

Full Name	Birth	Death	Age
Richard Smith	1903	1953	50
1.			
2.			
3.			
4.			
5.			
6.			
7.			
8.			

35

Group the ages of the people whose names have been recorded.

0–10 _____	51–60 _____
11–20 _____	61–70 _____
21–30 _____	71–80 _____
31–40 _____	81–90 _____
41–50 _____	

At what "age group" did most people die? _____

What could be a possible reason for this? _____

_____

GATHERING MORE INFORMATION

Residents from Other Lands

Name	Country
1.	
2.	
3.	
4.	
5.	

Our Stone Tally

Stone Type	Tally	Number
Granite		
Marble		
Limestone		
Concrete		
Other		

Epitaphs (sayings in stone in memory of the deceased):

1. _____

2. _____

3. _____

4. _____

5. _____

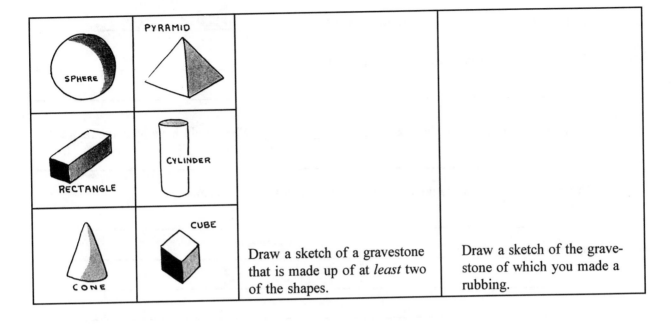

Draw a sketch of a gravestone that is made up of at *least* two of the shapes.

Draw a sketch of the gravestone of which you made a rubbing.

ORGANIZING! your results

1. What was the name of the oldest person whose stone was found?

   _____

2. What was the name of the youngest person whose stone was found?

   _____

3. What was the name of a soldier whose grave was found? _____

   _____ In what war? _____

   List below possible ways by which that soldier might have died.

   a. _____

   b. _____

4. What kind of rock or stone was most used for tombstones in the 1800's? _____

What might have been the reason for its use? _____

5.   What was the most unusual or interesting epitaph found? _____

_____

6.   In what year did many of the deaths occur? _____ What might have been the reason for

this? _____

List below some things to do and to remember when visiting a cemetery.

a.   _____

b.   _____

c.   _____

d.   _____

A Farm Visit

A visit to a farm can be an exciting learning experience for children at any age. For a farm to operate successfully, several important components must be brought together: (1) human skill and knowledge, (2) capital, (3) land and soil, (4) crops and livestock, (5) machinery and buildings, and (6) human labor. Children should know about such things.

A visit to a farm can help children to better understand what is involved in the production of their food, shelter, and clothing. This series of questions or activities is for upper-grade children who are completing an extensive unit on farming. Give each student or small group of students the responsibility for obtaining the answer to one or two of these questions or problems on the field trip and reporting back to the entire class.

1. Sketch the arrangement of the buildings, and have the farmer explain the reasons for this particular layout.

2. Measure the outside dimensions of the livestock buildings. Find how much space is allotted per cow, hog, or chicken.

3. Learn how many acres are needed to feed one cow. How many acres are in the entire farm?

4. How much is produced on this farm in the way of hogs, cattle, sheep, chickens, milk, eggs, grain, fruit, tobacco, etc.?

5. What is the cost per unit of product (dozen eggs, liter (gallon) of milk, etc.)? Compare the difference between the price the farmer gets for products and what you pay for them in the store. What is responsible for the difference?

6. Calculate the height of the silo. What is its capacity?

7. How is "run-off" prevented? How is soil fertility maintained?

8. Is there a woodlot? If so, what use is made of it?

9. Examine the barns, and note the details of the construction.

10. Collect seeds such as corn, wheat, and oats, and germinate them back in the classroom.

11. Find out if there is a relationship between "soil type" and crops that are grown.

12. What are the uses for the major plant crops grown on this farm?

13. What kinds of implements are used? Does the farmer own all the types and kinds of machinery needed?

14. Take some samples of soil and test them for pH, nitrogen, phosphorus, and potassium.

15. What breeds or types of animals and plants are raised on the farm? List some specific characteristics of each breed and variety.

16. What is "barnyard manure"? How is it removed from the barnyard? Is it returned to the soil? How and why?

17. What kinds of fertilizers are used? What is their cost? How much is used per acre?

18. What are herbicides and insecticides? List those that are used. How much of each is used per acre? How are they applied?

19. Is this a "family farm"? How long has this "family" owned it? Is "hired help" employed? Is there a son or daughter to continue with the farming operation? What education did (will) the son or daughter receive beyond high school?

20. In what ways has modern technology (a) increased productivity, (b) reduced the physical labor needed, and (c) increased the risk of farming?

21. In what ways are computers used on this farm?

22. What is done to avoid or reduce the amount of pollution on this farm?

23. What kind of bookkeeping system is used? Does the farmer keep the books?

24. Is this farmer a member of a cooperative (such as Farmers Union or American Farm Bureau Federation)?

25. Upon returning to the classroom:

    a. Develop a "farm booklet" in which you record the answers to these and similar questions.

    b. Develop a diagram to illustrate the significance of a small farm or industry like this to the economy of the community and to the nation.

    c. Invite the farmer to visit your classroom to discuss the follow-up activities.

    d. Invite local business owners to your classroom to discuss the importance of farming to their business and the overall community.

Investigate the Courthouse

Most governmental functions of counties or parishes in the United States are executed in, or near, the courthouse, and they are very important to us. The exact organization of county functions varies from state to state, even within a state. This is the reason that at least two visits to the courthouse are recommended:

1. Conduct a "scouting" trip to determine what offices are housed therein. This information can usually be found in a building directory on the first floor. Take a list of the offices and any descriptive material you can obtain back to the classroom for preliminary study.

2. Conduct a second (more if needed) trip, and focus attention on the functions of the different offices. Have the students help to prepare lists of questions to be answered.

Sample Questions

1. What does county government do?

2. What is the special job of the (a) tax collector, (b) sheriff, (c) judge, (d) county clerk, etc.?

3. What is the job of a county supervisor (or commissioner)?

4. Is there a county executive? If so, what duties does the executive perform? What title does the job carry?

5. What is the relationship between the sheriff's office and the local police department? The state police? The Federal Bureau of Investigation (FBI)?

6. Is the county jail a place in which you'd like to spend more time?

7. Is there township government in this county? If so, what do the township government officials do?

Depending upon the age of the students, their interests, and many other factors, the list of questions may become quite long, necessitating several trips; or it may be a rather brief, one-trip list. In either event, the questions should be used to direct a group interview with one or more of the county officials.

As a follow-up, students may want to do some of these:

1. Draw up an organizational chart depicting the structure and function of county government.

2. Write a story such as "A Day in the Sheriff's Life."

3. Make a flow chart of a tax bill from the county assessor's office through the actual payment by a citizen.

4. Write and perform a play about the duties of a selected county official.

Taping Oral History

The advent of low-priced, simple-to-operate tape recorders has brought oral history—once the exclusive domain of professional historians—into the realm of the possible for almost everyone. Armed with a portable tape recorder and a few carefully prepared "trigger" questions, a youngster can delve into the exciting business of first-hand historical research.

The following simple suggestions can help the neophyte historian get started:

1. Try out the tape recorder by practicing on friends. Become well acquainted with all of the controls.

2. Plan a brief explanation of what you plan to do and why. Your subject will appreciate it.

3. Record your first tape with someone you know rather well; this will make both of you more comfortable. Also make the first few tapings brief.

4. Encourage the subject to talk freely; do little talking yourself.

5. Begin with specific topics. Any one of these or similar topics can serve to "open-up" your subject and will probably suggest dozens of new topics to you.

   a. School-day memories
   b. Travel in the old days
   c. Farm life in the past
   d. City life in the past
   e. Old radio shows
   f. Favorite actors and actresses
   g. The Great Depression
   h. Favorite family foods
   i. Homemade toys

6. At the end of each recording session, make notes to guide your next one. Record what was successful and what wasn't in order to improve your technique. Make notes on new topics suggested by the previous taping.

7. Prepare a simple index of each tape cassette.

Study a Shopping Center

Shopping centers, the modern-day substitutes for the "country store," are an ever-increasing phenomenon in the urban landscape. Learning how they are organized, built, and operated makes an interesting research project.

Careful, detailed planning is required for the shopping center study because of their complex nature. Indeed, if the objective is that of learning about one of the massive modern centers, which is in many respects like a small city, it may be a good idea to do a "trial run" on a small center first. Choose a center with a dozen or fewer shops, study it carefully, and practice the research techniques needed before tackling the big job.

Whether studying small or large centers, students will need to prepare interview schedules because most of the needed information will come from people who work there. Here is a sample of the kinds of questions which should be posed:

1.   How many hectares (acres) does the center cover? How much land is devoted to parking lots? How much to buildings? How long has it been here?

2.   What materials were used in constructing the building(s)? In the parking lot?

3.   What retail outlets are represented? Can a family live entirely with goods purchased in the center? What items may not be available?

4.   What is the environmental impact of the center? On water run-off? On oxygen consumption? On transportation routes and traffic? Is noise and light pollution a problem?

5.   What has been the economic impact on "neighborhood" stores?

6.   How are the wastes generated at the center treated? Where do they go?

7.   How much—and what kinds of—energy is used daily? Monthly? Yearly? How much of this is used at the center? In transporting people and goods to the center?

8.   How many people work at the center? What are the qualifications for the jobs that are available?

9.   What has been the impact on the the neighborhood?

V. Ecological Studies

How we affect or impact the environment is one of the most important considerations we face. An awareness of the interdependence of the various elements that make up our planet must become an important part of everyone's education. Important in this are experiences outside the classroom where ecological "happenings" can be observed and studied first-hand.

Ecological studies may be undertaken at any location or place. Studies of the ecology of a city, with a human focus, is one form of them in which learners examine the relationship of people, industry, highways, waste disposal, institutions, natural resources, etc. Parks and vacant areas can be used as sites from which to study birds, insects, plants, and other forms of wildlife that may have adapted to urban conditions.

In "natural areas" resources are different and provide possibilities for other types of learning experiences. Studies may be made in such "areas" as are available and the life there compared with that in managed areas such as farms and nurseries.

The focus should center on a few basic ideas: (1) habitat, (2) adaptation, (3) succession, (4) food webs and chains, and (5) food pyramids. This section deals with some approaches teachers use.

Some Background

Habitat. Habitat consists of interacting factors such as plants, soil, rocks and minerals, available water, and climate. It is the home environment of living things. Major habitat areas include flowing or still waters, marshes, forests, fields, deserts, mountains, prairies, grasslands, and oceans. There may be many variations within each of these areas. Some plant and animal forms are very specialized and are able to survive in only one specific habitat type; other forms move freely from one condition to another. The edges of habitat zones generally contain a greater variety of life since the organisms from adjoining zones may also be present.

Adaptation. Each species has adapted to a way of life in its own habitat. Coloration enables animals to blend into their surroundings. Mouth and eyes serve specialized functions as does skin or outer covering. Special parts of plants absorb energy from the sun. Reproduction rates vary greatly among animals. Protective covering is vitally important to some animals to provide a shield from the weather and from their enemies.

Succession. Patterns of succession can be traced in many areas. When mature trees are removed, brush, fast-growing trees, shrubs, and grasses first flourish, only to be forced out later

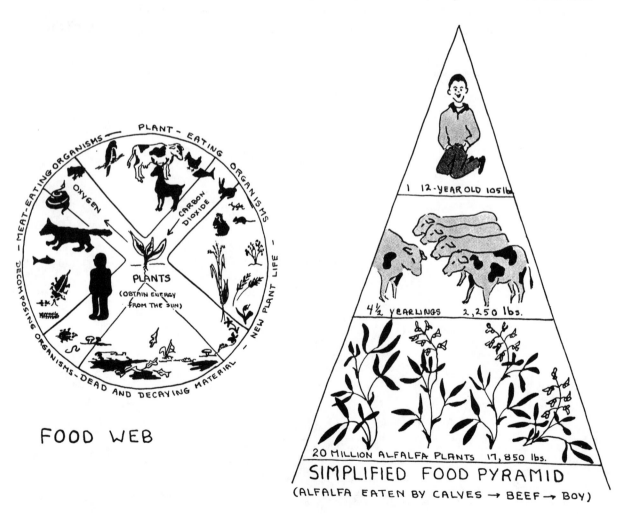

FOOD WEB

SIMPLIFIED FOOD PYRAMID
(ALFALFA EATEN BY CALVES → BEEF → BOY)

by more dominant and better adapted species. As food and cover change in these areas, animal forms appear and disappear through successive stages. The length of such stages varies considerably (from a year or so to several hundred years). Some disruptions lead to entirely new patterns of succession. Succession studies require that records be kept over a long period of time to note changes.

Food Webs. Food webs help to illustrate the intricacy of supply and demand for food. Simple plant life is the basis for sustaining all animal life and is the center of the web. Dead and decaying plants provide materials for other plants and animals, while living plants remove carbon dioxide from the air and give off oxygen. Tiny organisms feed on the plants and in turn are fed upon by larger animals. Even many large plant eaters are food for meat eaters. Some life forms (such as parasites) live within larger organisms. Insects eat other insects and other "bugs" and in turn are eaten by others. By observing the overlapping of food supply, we form the "web."

Food Pyramids. The food pyramid is a way to illustrate differences in size and numbers of different forms of life at the different parts of the food web or chain. It helps to illustrate the differences in size, numbers, reproductive rate, and the relationships between "consumers" and "producers" of food. The base of the pyramid consists of micro-organisms (mostly plants) and builds to the peak where one finds only consumers and predators.

Habitat Studies

Habitat might be explained as the home of a living thing. Habitats are of many forms such as deserts, oceans, rivers, lakes, marshes, grasslands, forests, and swamps. Within each of these are many sub-forms. Among the major components of habitat are factors such as water, weather, climate, and land composition.

Habitat is an important concept in ecological studies as living things are adapted to one or more habitat forms. If their habitat is disturbed, the inter-relationships of the organisms there are disrupted, and the ensuing "ripple" can have long-range implications that extend far beyond the affected area. *Humans are notorious as habitat disrupters* who greatly affect all life forms.

Some have called Lake Erie a "dead lake" because of pollution. Oil seepage has destroyed marine life along certain coastal areas, and years may pass before the normal balance is reached. Pollution of the air appears to be destroying other forms of life in urban habitats. Some fear that the changes we are making throughout the earth's total atmosphere are affecting living things in a major way.

Farming practices result in other changes. Pesticides used to protect agricultural crops destroy the natural predators of these pests, thus creating the need for more chemical controls. This then affects other forms of life—birds, fish, insects, mammals, etc. Because such problems persist and will increase in importance, children need to understand ecological relationships and to gain more knowledge about *habitat.*

Make the school and nearby community the beginning point of this understanding. Find different types of habitats and study them. On most school sites, these include blacktop, concrete, gravel, grass, exposed soil, ditches, shrubs, flowers, trees, etc. Examine the kinds of life found in each area. Are some types found in several of these "micro-habitats"? After exploring the readily visible areas, look below the surface to find other forms (parts of plants, worms, insects etc.). Place a sheet of newspaper under the branches of shrubs and trees and shake them to see what drops off. Examine the cracks of concrete and blacktop surfaces and the bark and leaves of trees and other plants to see what lives there.

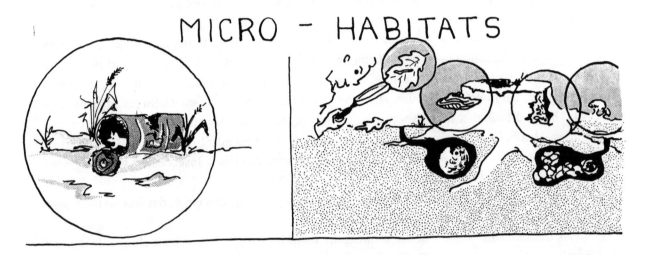

MICRO - HABITATS

When studying in major habitat formations, such as forests and fields, develop the concept of "edge." Edge areas contain life forms that can subsist in either habitat or can use both. Edge areas are actually additional forms of habitats with their own unique forms of life.

Take a small area (square meter/square foot) and disturb it to learn what happens over a period of a few days, weeks, or months. Does it return to its original state, or does it undergo significant changes that appear to be permanent?

Weather studies should also be included when examining habitats. Notice the differences in temperature and light intensity in the various areas. Where are the cooler spots, the warmer spots, and so on? At what temperature and moisture ranges do you observe the greatest amount of plant growth? The greatest amount of animal activity?

Adaptation Studies

The adaptive ability of any species is a critical factor in its survival. Disruption of habitats directly affects food and shelter for living things and leads to changes in their very forms of life. Major changes often result in severe depletion or extinction of species. Other species readily adapt and survive.

The ways that living things have adapted to various habitat types are evident. The breathing apparatus of aquatic forms remove oxygen from the water; whereas, many land animals can obtain oxygen only from the air. Many amphibians and insects move from one habitat to another in the course of their life cycle.

Predators can usually be distinguished by the set of their eyes, mouth, and teeth. Their eyes are set forward, enabling them to focus on objects that are ahead, and their teeth and mouth are most efficient for grasping and tearing. Birds with comparatively slender beaks are generally predators that eat insects, frogs, fish, etc. They have sharp talons that are useful for grasping and a solid hooked beak that facilitates tearing. The size, shape and location of the mouth of a fish signifies what it eats. Bottom feeders usually have rounded mouths located in the lower part of the skull facing down, with eye location facilitating downward vision. Insect eaters generally have small mouths. Fish that eat other fish have large mouths.

Moles live underground and "swim" through the soil using special large, flat feet well-adapted for digging. Moles, like worms, lack functional eyes.

Ask questions like these when examining the footprints of animals: Can it climb? Is it a fast runner? Can it grasp and tear? Was it walking or running or loping? Is it a nimble, graceful animal, or is it awkward? Is it a good swimmer?

Protective coloration is vitally important to the survival of some animals. The female of most bird species is dull and drab—a type of protection while it is on the nest. Deer, rabbits, and mice are extremely difficult to see when they stand still in their natural habitat. Some animals that are defenseless resemble others that are well-armed or distasteful.

Some species can range through a wide variety of habitats; hence, they are found in many places. On the other hand, some species require a very specialized habitat and diet. The kite hawk and the arctic grayling are among such forms.

When examining plant and animal life, carefully note the location and surroundings where each species was seen. Examine (if possible) to see what the animal eats and how well it is adapted to its surroundings—and learn to recognize what will happen to it when that relationship is changed.

A Fact Sheet for the Study of a Micro-habitat

Schoolyards often seem like sterile places for ecological studies. However, the study of a micro-habitat is an ideal activity for a schoolyard; it requires little space and encourages students to carefully examine both the commonplace and the familiar. Have students work in pairs or teams. Throw a Frisbee® or Hula-Hoop® in a random direction in the area to determine the location and size of the micro-habitat to be studied. The location is determined by where the tossed article lands. The size is determined by the circumference of the area covered by the Frisbee® or Hula-Hoop®. Have the students examine it carefully and compare their findings with those of the other students studying different micro-habitats.

1. What is the dominant plant? _____

   About how many of these plants are there? _____

   What percentage of the area do they cover? _____

2. List all other plants in the plot. _____

   _____

   How many are there? _____

   What percentage of the area do they cover? _____

3. What animals are present? _____

   How many of each? _____

4. Examine the soil and describe it. _____

   What indications of human interference can you find? _____

   _____

5. Name the plot. _____

6. How will this area look in a year? _____

   In five years? _____

7. What can you do to improve or preserve the area? Discuss this in class.

A Fact Sheet for a Changing Forest Edge

This is an interesting activity in which you collect data about a "forest edge" (where a forest and adjacent field meet). Lay out a line transect, using a rope or string, in which one end is located about 10 meters (10 yards) inside the edge of a forest and the other extends about the same distance into the adjoining field. Mark off intervals (meters or yards) along the line, and take measurements at appropriate locations along the line:

1. Identify and count all trees which have branches that are within 1 meter (1 yard) of the line. _____

   _____

2. Identify and count all shrubs with branches within 1 meter (1 yard) of the line.

   _____

   _____

3. Identify and count herbaceous plants growing within 1 meter (1 yard) of the line.

   _____

   _____

4. Identify and count animals that are in or pass through an area within 1 meter (1 yard) of the line. _____

   _____

5. Name the plots. (Usually, ecosystems are named after the predominant plant or vegetation.) _____

   _____

6. Compare results along the transect.

7. Which plots have the greatest diversity of plant life? _____
   Of animal life? _____

8. If undisturbed, how might this area look in five years? _____
   In 10 years? _____

The Predator–Prey Game

Objective: Predator–Prey is a game to increase interest in animals and to develop children's understanding of animal behavior.

It deals with questions such as "How do animals protect themselves?" and "Why do animals make sounds?"

The game is played after dark in a clear area with a few trees and shrubs for hiding places. The size of the area depends upon the size of the group—generally about 20 children require a 70- × 30-meter (225- × 100-foot) area. The game is played in three phases.

All that is needed for equipment is a multiple set of sound-making devices. Natural items such as rocks or pieces of wood struck against each other make good sounds. Rubber bands wrapped around wooden blocks and snapped against the wood can be used. Two wooden blocks with sandpaper glued around them and rubbed together are good. Purchased horns and whistles make interesting sounds. Anything that makes a unique sound works.

Phase I

Equipment needed: An even number of each sound-making device:
(20 players)
        Four wooden blocks with a rubber band around each one.
        Four pairs of sandpaper blocks.
        Four pairs of rocks.
        Four horns.
        Four whistles.

Directions: Have the players form a circle facing away from the center with their hands behind their backs. Give each player one sound-making device. When these have been distributed, instruct the players to scatter throughout the area and hide. At a prearranged signal by you, have them begin to make sounds for another "animal" making a similar sound. When they find their "partner," have them return to where they started.

During this first phase, every player will find a partner. When they have all returned to their home base, discuss the reasons that animals make sounds. Mate attraction, territorial defense, and warning signals are a few of the ideas to discuss.

Phase II

Equipment needed: An uneven number of each sound-making device:
(20 players)
        Five wooden blocks with a rubber band around each one.

Five pairs of sandpaper blocks.
Five pairs of rocks.
Five whistles.

Directions: Repeat the procedure followed in Phase I except that this time hand out an uneven number of each type of sound-making device. Explain that all players will not find partners and that when you signal, they should return to the starting point, even if they do not have a partner.

When they are all at home base, discuss the reasons all animals do not find mates. For example, animal mortality caused by hunting deaths, roadside accidents, disease, etc. To illustrate further, use the example of small populations of whales spread over large areas.

Phase III

Equipment needed: An even number of each sound-making device (four less than number of
(20 players)   players):
                    Four wooden blocks with a rubber band around each one.
                    Four pairs of sandpaper blocks.
                    Four pairs of rocks.
                    Four whistles.

Directions: Repeat the procedure followed in Phases I and II except that this time make four of the players "predators" by only touching their hands when distributing the sound-making devices to the other players who are the "prey." Instruct the predators to catch their prey by tagging them and to devise methods other than running them down to catch them. Inform the prey that if they find partners and can return to home base with their partner before being tagged, they are safe.

After all the players have returned to home base, discuss the methods used by the predators to catch their prey. Relate this to the actual methods employed by predators of the animal world. Discuss the methods of escape used by the prey who survived and the mistakes made by those who were tagged. Lead the discussion into the reasons that predators are important in a natural environment.

When the game and discussions are finished, conduct a night hike to focus attention on sound sensitivity.

Back in the classroom, supervise a study of the various aspects of animal behavior.

NOTE: Be sure that none of the sound-making devices can injure the chidren if they should fall while running. For example, do *not* use long horns during Phase III.

VI. Studies of Environmental Impact

The current environmentalism now assures that (1) the air, water, and land can no longer be used indiscriminately and (2) the outcomes of use must be known in advance and requests submitted to the proper authorities before permission to proceed is received.

We no longer accept the notion that the rivers, oceans, and seas are a "commons" into which wastes are spewed. Although there are many people who have never accepted this idea, they now have the backing of a variety of environmental protection acts and agencies, all of which are supported by public opinion.

Until recently, individuals and government could move ahead as they wished and make the changes they wanted to make, heedless, of the long-term consequences. But this is no longer true, and much of what they want to do must now meet the test of public scrutiny.

The result is the creation of several new environmental professions to (1) project the environmental impact for those who would make a change and (2) represent the environment and the public in the review of such projections.

Herein lie excellent teaching opportunities: (1) the review of actual Environmental Impact Statements and (2) the development of real or simulated Environmental Impact Statements.

This section should be helpful to teachers who wish to deal with this form of public participation. The first page provides a bit of background information. Guidesheets, suggested problems and approaches for study, and other tips follow.

Environmental Impact Statements—The Idea

The United States Environmental Protection Act requires completion of an Environmental Impact Statement (EIS) before decisions to proceed are made about *major* projects that involve federal permits, funds, or personnel. Several states have enacted legislation that requires the completion of similar Environmental Impact Statements on projects requiring state permits, funds, and personnel.

Environmental Impact Statements are available for review by interested persons, including teachers and students. Copies are placed in libraries near the location of proposed projects for the use of those who are interested. Copies are sent to environmental protection agencies (EPA's) at the regional and federal levels, and they have staff members who review these statements.

Persons concerned about (1) the thoroughness of the impact statement or (2) insufficient attention being given to the areas of impact revealed by the study may ask for and get public hearings. At these, the proposer is required to answer questions and respond to challenges regarding the impact of their proposed projects. Decisions subsequently may be made about the project or the EIS by the judiciary. Such decisions may range from allowing the project to go ahead as proposed, to amending the project or the EIS, or to entirely abandoning the project.

The purpose of the EIS process is not to halt progress, as many of its critics claim. It is to require an examination beforehand rather than to learn about the problems "too late." Such examinations frequently result in the modification of a proposal to make it more environmentally sound and more in accord with corporate and public needs.

The key to the process is public participation. Little is gained by spending much time and money developing EIS's if they (1) lie unexamined on library shelves and (2) are not used even by developers in their decision-making.

Teachers, particularly those of high school courses on contemporary problems, have an opportunity and an obligation to apprise their students of this important process and how they might become an important part of the nation's decision-making process.

A flaw or weakness in the process, as yet unresolved, has to do with knowing what is or is not "major" and the extent to which certain governmental and public agencies are exempt from the requirements of completing environmental impact studies. Hence, some projects get by without the proper review.

A visit to nearby public libraries should reveal what is available in the way of Environmental Impact Statements and the projects currently being considered locally. Copies, for school use, can occasionally be obtained from project proposers or from the EPA regional offices—they sometimes receive more copies than they need and will donate them.

Reviewing an Environmental Impact Statement

Obtain copies of an Environmental Impact Statement on a nearby project of interest to your students. Examine it carefully and carry out your own review of the project.

Consider: A visit to the actual site so that students can visually check what is being proposed and determine its impact on the area.

Arranging interviews or class visits by representatives of the agency proposing the change, and (to provide balance) those opposing the project.

Deal with questions like these about the project:

1. What is being proposed? What changes are being made?

2. Why is this to be done? What needs will be met by this project? What problems will it help to solve? What are the benefits?

3. Who is responsible for the project? Is a government agency(s) involved? In what way are private individuals or corporations involved?

4. What is the connection between who is proposing the project and the problem it addresses (2 above)?

5. Is the Environmental Impact Statement clear? What is the short-term environmental impact? What is the long-term impact? Was a thorough job done to assess environmental impact? Are there some areas that were not considered that may be environmentally significant? Is the impact overstated? Understated?

6. What is the economic impact of the project? (Lately the economic impact of a proposed project has been considered in making these studies.) Is the effect of this project likely to be less than or more than the benefits to be derived from it?

7. Have the alternatives been thoroughly considered? What are these alternatives and why were they rejected?

8. What is your position? Is the Environmental Impact Statement adequate? Should the project be permitted to move forward? If your answer is "no," what changes might be made to make it acceptable to you?

9. What will we do? What is our role? What steps should we take? Is it appropriate for us to request a hearing?

Let's Do an Environmental Impact Study

Assign this as a term project. Have the students work individually, in teams, or as an entire class. Set as their goal an in-depth study of a project being proposed in the community or on the school site to gather information and answers that would enable decision-makers to make a reasonable determination in assessing the environmental impact and the benefits to be derived from the project.

Have the students submit an Environmental Impact Statement in which they do the following:

1. Carefully describe what is to be done. Be as precise as possible in identifying the location, any construction that will be done, and all alterations to be made.

2. Determine, in addition to that which is to be done on-site, what other changes or ripples will result in the general area (e.g., constructing a shopping center is likely to result in a change in nearby traffic patterns and possibly result in a need for new highways).

3. Describe the existing situation. What now occupies the site? How is it used? What uses will no longer be possible? Look at the broad picture in dealing with this question. Perhaps the site appears to have no use except as a home for mice and to serve as a sponge during rainfalls. This may be important!

4. Explain the purpose of the proposed change. Whom will it benefit or serve? In what ways will they be served? What is the rationale? Is it being designed to meet a private need, a public need, or both?

5. Contrast the physical environment at the present time with that once the project is completed. What is the impact of the project on this area? On the surrounding area? What will be changed?

6. Investigate the impact on the fauna and flora. What life forms will gain? What life forms will lose? To what extent will they gain and lose? Is this significant?

7. Consider what might be the objections to this project and who are likely to object. On what basis will they object?

8. Determine if this project appears to be economically viable. Are the benefits to the individual and the public likely to be as great as the cost? Take environmental cost into consideration as well.

9. Express your point-of-view concerning this project. Is it environmentally, economically, and morally sound? Does it make sense?

10. Set forth any appropriate alternatives. Designate those that seem most viable. On the surface, what appears to be more acceptable about your alternatives than the original project? What appears to be less acceptable?

11. Clarify your position on the project. Should it move forward? Should it be altered? Should it be dropped? If it should be altered, what changes do you propose?

Environmental Impact Studies: Using Simulated Proposals

If you are lacking a real, down-to-earth, live proposal for your students to study, you may wish to develop your own "simulated proposals." Before doing so, however, carefully look for real proposals to change things around the school. A short conference with most administrators (and many teachers) will reveal a number of ideas for changing things—some which have been shelved, some which are presently in the works.

We know of some instances in which an environmental impact study by students resulted in a "dusty" proposal being brought forth and implemented. And, we know of others in which very live proposals were buried because of the impact study.

There is big advantage, however, to using simulated proposals for environmental impact studies. These can be designed and selected to fit specific educational interests and needs. Here are a few "simulated proposals" applicable to many situations:

1. To remove the hedge and row of trees that shade the primary wing.

2. To make the street in front of the school one-way.

3. To convert the teacher's parking lot to tennis courts, or, as is more often done, to change the tennis courts to a parking area.

4. To propose that a fast-food restaurant locate across the street from the high school.

5. To level the playground to provide for better drainage.

6. To add 10 meters (33 feet) to the length of the multi-purpose room.

7. To enclose (or fence) the school grounds—making them available only during school hours.

8. To enclose (or fence) the fourth and last open side of the courtyard.

9. To till a portion of the school lawn to provide the fourth graders with a place for their garden.

10. To add storm windows to the third-floor windows.

11. To place a bird feeder outside the third-grade windows.

12. To place a bicycle rack outside the school office window and require that all bicycles be parked there.

13. To change the school mowing program—perhaps by discontinuing mowing entirely on selected portions of the school site.

Proposals or topics that might be more appropriate for environmental impact studies at the resident outdoor education center or camp are:

1. To remove the "brush" and small trees from the acreage on which the camp buildings are located and keep it mowed—largely as a security and fire control measure.

2. To construct several (two or three) small cabins at appropriate locations in the woods—to serve as pioneer stations for more advanced students.

3. To "blacktop" an area near the dining hall so as to have a suitable area for volleyball and other sports.

4. To construct and operate a year-round bird-feeding station near the visitor's center.

5. To let the open field revert to forest.

6. To implement a management program for the "stream" passing through the camp in which the banks are straightened, the bottom is dredged, and the overhanging trees and shrubs are removed.

Another type of problem often posed by social studies teachers and similar to these proposals for environmental change deal with, "What would happen if . . .?" Students are instructed to conduct extensive research to try to determine or predict the results of a proposed change. Examples of this type are:

1. What would happen if the world population stopped growing?

2. What would happen if the environmental protection agencies were abolished.

3. What would happen if the OPEC nations refused to sell oil to us?

4. What would happen if the "pristine" area near town was designated as a state park?

5. What would happen if we all were guided by an environmental conscience?

6. What would happen if we had to pay twice as much for electricity consumed during peak periods as for other periods?

VII. Geology and Soils

Children at every age level can participate in outdoor studies which deal with nearby soils, rocks, and landforms. Most children are fascinated by the rocks and pebbles they find, and these resources can help reach many educational objectives. With sufficient understanding, their interest often grows, and their "rock collections" become the focus of reading and study far beyond what one might ordinarily expect from a particular age level.

In some cases the rocks, pebbles, and soils on the school grounds or campsite may be the only readily accessible source of such materials. These should be used to the maximum extent. Usually, however, hills and valleys with accompanying deposits of soil, gravel, and outcroppings of bedrock can be found nearby. Forest preserves, parks, and campsites are often rich in resources for geology and soils study. These sites are often available simply because their terrain is too uneven and hilly for other uses.

Focus on: (1) using the resources at hand that the children know and (2) involving them in as many direct experiences as possible. Basically, such studies will be more interesting to children if the focus is on the rocks, soils, and geologic history of the area in which they live rather than areas hundreds of miles away about which they can read but never see. Discovering a 300-million-year-old fossil or climbing down a hill and realizing that each step takes one back a million years in time can have a tremendous impact on anyone, especially when it's in your own backyard.

Obviously, teachers must have some familiarity with the geology and soils of the area in which they work. Further help can be obtained locally from (1) soil conservation and agricultural extension services, (2) science teachers in nearby high schools, and (3) staff at nearby colleges.

The material in this section has been used in working with children as well as with university students. Some of it was designed to provide users with background. Some is method-oriented and provides activities and techniques to be used with students. Hopefully, it will provide a source of ideas that users can modify to meet their own needs.

Field Experiences to Include in a Geology Unit

Objectives: To help students:

Understand about the origin of rocks, minerals, and landforms.

Clarify their understanding of geologic change and enhance their appreciation of the forces that effect change.

Develop attitudes and appreciations about the relationships in geology.

Extend their concepts of geologic time.

Preparation: Pupils should know and understand geologic terms such as rocks, minerals, rock strata, landforms, etc. They should know the explanations for these items and something about the causes of geologic change.

Pupils should know how local rocks and minerals are used by humans and of the relationships between humans and these materials.

Equipment:

Rock hammers	Hardness testing materials
Lenses	Streak plates
Dilute HCl or "strong vinegar"	Reference specimens
Collecting bags	Appropriate references
Safety goggles	Identification keys

Activities:

1. *Examine nearby landforms with your students.*

   a. Develop understanding of these surface features first-hand.

   b. Categorize and name the local landforms.

   c. Propose hypotheses about the processes that caused them. Analyze the hypotheses.

   d. Offer predictions about changes (and rate of change) to occur in these forms and the eventual outcomes. Consider the forces (biotic and abiotic) that act upon them. Are humans accelerating the change? Is this "good"?

2. *Examine the outcrops and bedrock exposures in your area.*

   a. Notice the layering if any is evident; the slope or tilt of the layers; faulting; fossils; materials at each level and their characteristics (color, hardness, reaction to acid, minerals, structure, etc.).

   b. Propose explanations for the presence or absence of layering, faulting, hard and soft materials, types of fossils, time intervals, etc.

c.   Locate evidence of (and explanations for) weathering and erosion such as talus and wedging, primary plant succession, root fracturing, soil build-up, and concentration of more durable components such as chert.

d.   Visit quarries or mines to learn first-hand how rock and mineral materials are obtained, processed, and used.

e.   If you are in a heavily glaciated region with thick overlying layers of glacial drift, then outcroppings of rock may not be readily available for study. However, studying the effects of the glacier on the region may provide a very rewarding outdoor exercise. Collect glacial erratics (rocks brought in from a far distant place and not native to the particular area.) Visit nearby glacial deposits of gravel and sand.

3.   *Collect specimens of different types and kinds of rocks:*

a.   Fracture specimens and examine them carefully. Identify the differences and similarities and classify them accordingly.

b.   Construct keys, clue charts, or displays of the rocks you collect.

c.   Determine the origins of the rocks you collect. Learn when, where, and how they were formed.

d.   Identify and explain any fossils that you find.

e.   Make your own "fossils" in the classroom using plaster of Paris for imprinting shells, tracks, and other objects.

Landforms or Surface Features

Landforms are geologic features such as valleys, gullies, cliffs, deltas, fans, moraines, and dunes. They are of interest to geologists because they result from the action of various forces, and interesting relationships can be found between the fauna and flora and the physical and chemical characteristics of an area. Social scientists, on the other hand, may be more interested in the influence of these landforms on the history, development, and economy of the human inhabitants.

Children's understanding of geologic processes may be substantially improved through field experiences in

which they examine, sketch, and analyze nearby landforms. Teachers can frequently find miniature forms to assist students to understand the larger, more important geologic situations described in textbooks. For instance, a deposit of alluvium where a rapidly flowing tributary enters a slow river may help to illustrate *delta formation,* or the meanders of a small stream may help to illustrate the changes that occur with larger, more mature rivers.

Some Examples of Landforms to Study

Rills and Gullies. Some of the moisture that falls to the earth is quickly absorbed into the soil. The excess, however, gathers into small rivulets and eventually into streams as it moves to lower elevations. In doing so, it picks up soil and rock particles and sculptures the land. At first, rills a few centimeters (inches) in width and depth develop. After decades (though sometimes only in a matter of days) rills develop into gullies many meters (feet) in depth. Eventually, great valleys form.

Deltas. Where a river or stream enters a lake or sea it slows and the load of soil and rock particles it carries is deposited as a delta. Some of the great deltas (Mississippi, Nile, Amazon) are of great importance. Delta-like deposits occasionally accumulate where a small, rapidly-flowing stream enters a slow-moving river. These have many of the characteristics of real deltas and can be useful in teaching about deltas, soil movement, and deposition.

Alluvial Fans. The particles that a small, rapid-flowing stream carries as it cuts a gully into a hillside are deposited when the water slows at the gully mouth. This deposit of material, usually fan-shaped with channels cut through it, is called an alluvial fan.

Evidence of Stream Action. As water moves through a gully channel, its pounding results in the dislodgment of particles on the banks. Some of these particles are carried away in solution, and some are suspended. The larger particles roll along on the bottom, however. Wherever there is a bend in the channel, the water and its load strikes hardest at the concave (outer) sides of the channel, then slows and swirls to the convex (inner) sides with cutting and meandering as a result. The shifting of these meanders as the stream matures results in the formation of a broad flood plain composed of alluvial deposits.

These may help:

1. Aerial stereo-photographs and stereoscopes. These enable students to have three-dimensional views of landforms as seen from the air. They can be extremely effective as teaching aids and are available from suppliers such as Wards, Forestry Suppliers, and Nasco.

2. The *Set of One Hundred Topographic Maps* (or the smaller selection of twenty-five maps) the Geologic Survey of the U.S. Department of the Interior can be used to illustrate the variety in the U.S. physiographic features. Several of these maps are overprinted so as to accentuate the relief they illustrate.

3. Several companies, including those mentioned previously, also have landforms or surface features made of plastic that illustrate various features. They can be helpful in supplementing the field study of the local landforms.

Some Rock and Mineral Characteristics

Hardness: Rocks and minerals vary greatly in hardness. A specimen can be scratched with the sharp edge of a harder mineral if enough pressure is applied. On Mohs' scale, the hardest mineral is number 10, the softest is number 1.

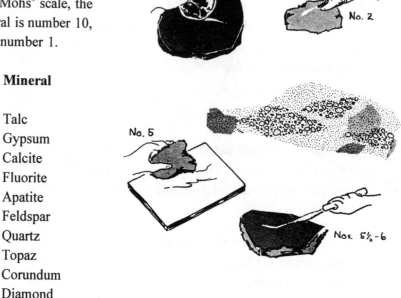

Hardness	Mineral
1	Talc
2	Gypsum
3	Calcite
4	Fluorite
5	Apatite
6	Feldspar
7	Quartz
8	Topaz
9	Corundum
10	Diamond

A thumbnail will scratch No. 2. A penny will scratch No. 3. Glass scratches No. 5. A good knife blade has a hardness of 5½ to 6. Impure minerals vary in hardness.

Color: Color is usually due to the light reflecting from the specimen. Some rocks, such as fluorite, quartz, granite, calcite, orthoclase, chert or flint, bauxite, and kaolin, may have several colors. Some rock specimens contain 20 or more kinds of minerals.

Luster: The luster of a rock or mineral depends upon its composition and the quality and intensity of the light reflected from its surface. Terms used to describe luster include: metallic, non-metallic, glassy, silky, pearly, dull or earthy, resinous, greasy, and brilliant.

Streak: Streak is the color of the mark a specimen makes when rubbed across a porcelain or streak plate. The streak is not always the same color as the specimen.

Cleavage: The tendency of some minerals to break along smooth planes in definite directions is called cleavage. Some minerals have several cleavage planes while other minerals have none.

Fracture: When specimens having no cleavage are broken, the break is usually irregular and is called a fracture. Some fractures (called conchoidal) tend to have surfaces that are irregularly curved in or cut.

Specific Gravity: The specific gravity of a rock or mineral is its weight as compared to the weight of an equal volume of water. Quartz approximates an average specific gravity for minerals.

Crystal Form: When pure, many rocks or minerals crystallize into definite forms or geometric arrangements. Crystals are easy to recognize, but care should be exerted to not confuse cleavage with crystal form.

Constructing a Rock Key

Objectives: To help students to recognize differences and similarities among rocks and to clarify understanding of the organization of knowledge.

Procedure: Instruct the students:

1. To go outdoors to collect rocks individually or in small groups. (Young children need to collect only four or five different kinds of rocks; older children will want to collect more.)

2. To sort their rocks, placing all like specimens together. To select a typical or "type" specimen from each group and mark it with a numeral assigned to the group.

3. To closely examine the "type" specimens and find a characteristic to divide them into two groups. To record this description at "A" in an outline and list those that fit this description (see "Example Key"). To record an opposite condition at "AA" and list the remaining "type" specimens. To question why they *must* meet this condition.

4. To work first with the "A" specimens to identify a characteristic to divide them into two groups. To record this at "B" and the alternative under "BB" (all under the heading "A"). To continue until only one "type" specimen is in each group. To repeat the above with the specimens placed in the "AA" group.

5. To check by selecting a specimen from one of the original piles and working it through the key. To ask, "Does it fit with the appropriate 'type' specimen?" and "Are they the same?" To repeat the procedure with several other specimens.

6. To assign descriptive names to replace the identifying numerals or marks by using a procedure similar to that used to give objects a name (see "Examining and Naming Specimens" on page 70). To exchange specimens and keys with their classmates to find out if they can identify each other's rocks by using the key.

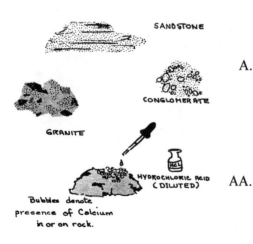

SANDSTONE

CONGLOMERATE

GRANITE

HYDROCHLORIC ACID (DILUTED)

Bubbles denote presence of Calcium in or on rock.

Example Key

A. Grain structure can be seen with eye. (1, 2, 4)
   B. Salt and pepper pattern—several colors. (2)
   BB. Only one color present. (1, 4)
      C. Light colored and glassy. (4)
      CC. Not as in "C." (1)

AA. No particles or crystals are visible. (3, 6)
   B. Bubbles when treated with acid. (3)
   BB. Doesn't bubble when treated. (6)

Let's Make Rock Collections

Children like to "collect," and rock collections can motivate learning. You may wish to start your students on individual collections or on a class, school, or camp collection in which each child contributes specimens obtained from nearby and distant places.

So often, however, children's rock collections are no more than accumulations of unlabeled and unknown specimens in a cardboard box. Obviously, the value of such collections is small, and interest in them dwindles.

The following may help you to use "rock collecting" to serve to (1) create interests about the world in which we live, (2) provide experiences with scientific methods and approaches, (3) stimulate the use of reference materials, (4) develop interests and understandings in geography and geology, and (5) create awareness of the surroundings.

*Finding
Specimens:*   Specimens may be obtained from many places. The school grounds, roadcuts, excavations, stream banks or dry stream beds, beaches, hillsides, eroded areas or quarries, and mine entrances are just a few.

Labeling: When specimens are found, they should be immediately marked and labeled. One technique is to carry a supply of small plastic bags, each identified by a number. The specimens should be placed individually in the bags, and the following data recorded in a log or field book: (1) specimen bag number; (2) name of person finding the specimen; (3) date the specimen was collected; (4) state, county, and nearest city or town where found; (5) vicinity and surroundings where found; and (6) other seemingly pertinent information.

At a later time the students will need to make permanent labels for each specimen containing its name as well as the above information. One technique is to paint a small area on the specimen. When this is dry, an identifying number can be painted on it. This provides an easy and reliable way to match label and specimen should they become separated.

*Storage and
Display:*   Cases in which to store and display rock collections vary from egg cartons (suitable for small pebbles collected by small children) to large, glass-topped specimen cases and boxes purchased from hobby and science supply firms. Each specimen should be placed in an individual compartment of a shallow box composed of only one layer. Display boxes may also be constructed of plywood or masonite with the compartments made of cardboard strips. Sliding plastic tops may be provided if 3-millimeter (⅛- to 3⁄16-inch) grooves are cut into the wood with a power saw before the box is assembled.

Examining
and Naming
Specimens: Encourage the children to examine their specimens, closely noting each character-istic, difference, and similarity (see "Some Rock and Mineral Characteristics" on page 66 for brief descriptions). They may wish to classify their rocks according to hardness, how and where formed, shape, color, uses, etc. Ultimately, they may want to identify and name their specimens. Simple rock keys, commercial rock collections, geology reference books, etc., will be needed for this purpose. Persons in local rock or lapidary clubs may help and often will come to school to work with children who are attempting to identify and name specimens.

Extend the
Collection: Organize a swap club in your class, camp, or school for the exchange of specimens.

Take a field trip to a rock and mineral show or to a nearby college or university to see rock collections.

Make your own rock collection (a teaching collection).

Other Things
to Learn:
1.   Do we use this rock or mineral for any commercial purpose? Is it "good" for anything?

2.   Where and when were these rocks originally formed? What was it like on the earth at that time?

3.   How was this rock transported to where it was found?

4.   Investigate careers that deal with rocks (such as geology, mining, or concrete work).

Soil Studies

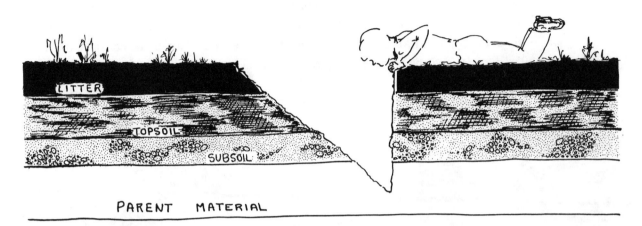

LITTER

TOPSOIL

SUBSOIL

PARENT MATERIAL

Take students to a nearby field to examine several examples of soil through direct, first-hand experiences. A useful site for a study area would be a cultivated spot on the school grounds or campsite, a nearby park or woodlot, a new excavation, or a farm field. It is helpful if you have background information about each site which includes (1) the depth of the soil, (2) the slope, (3) the vegetative cover, (4) a history of use, and (5) the previous treatment. Samples of various kinds of soil may be taken back into the classroom or laboratory for additional study.

Area soil conservation service personnel and the agricultural extension agent are usually willing to assist with soil studies. Some activities that have been useful to teachers follow:

Sensory Examination of a Soil

Overview: Before undertaking an activity, have the students scan the site from several directions. Get the "lay of the land" from their descriptions. If there is no excavation at the site, make one using a shovel or spade. Cut to a depth that exposes the various soil layers, usually about 30 to 60 centimeters (1 to 2 feet). Cut one side of the hole straight up and down, and slope the other side.

NOTE: If you think you will need assistance in digging the hole, send an assistant to prepare the site before the activity.

Handling the Soil: Have each student take a handful of soil from each of several depths and "squeeze and ball" it, attempting to form a "ribbon" between the fingers and thumb, as a test of the plasticity and moisture content. The finer the particles, the easier it is to ribbon (clay-like soils ribbon very easily). Instruct one or two students to describe the sensations such as which feels the wettest, stickiest, or coldest. "Taste" and smell the samples and make comparisons.

The

Profile: Scrape the steep side of the "cut" to insure a smooth surface for examination; then have measurements and sketches made of the soil "profile." Include descriptions about the color, thickness of layers, size of particles, etc. Notice the consistency of the material and the presence of various material such as roots and rocks.

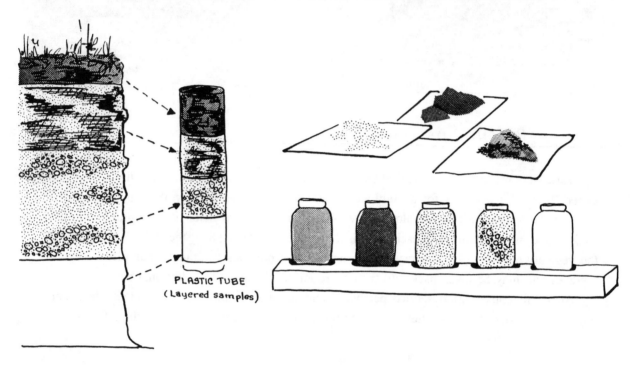

PLASTIC TUBE
(Layered samples)

Organic

Matter: Have the students examine the layers for evidences of organic matter. Are both undecayed and decayed materials present? Where are they found? Is there evidence of insects? What is the extent of the penetration of roots and insects? Is there any non-soil material present? Describe it and explain how it got there.

Study the Physical and Chemical Characteristics of Soil

Texture: Dry a sample of the soil and break it into fine particles (using a mortar and pestle or roller on a board).

   1.   Pass this material through various sizes of screens. Examine that which is retained on each screen for sharpness of edges, shape, color, and the way each particle is broken (use a hand lens or a low-powered microscope).

   2.   Fill a small jar about two-thirds full of water. Add powdered soil until the jar is full. Cap, shake vigorously, and allow to settle. Measure the layers. Do small particles require more time to settle than larger particles? (Adding one-fourth teaspoon of alum and a teaspoon of household ammonia helps to speed the process.) Examine the material at each layer.

Organic Content: Generally, the higher the organic content the better the soil is agriculturally.

   1.   Trim away the above-ground vegetation where the sample is to be taken. Take a sample about $15 \times 15 \times 15$ centimeters ($6 \times 6 \times 6$ inches) in size and spread it out on newspapers so that each student has a portion. Carefully separate the material into (a) plant matter such as sticks, leaves, and roots; (b) animal life such as worms, grubs, etc.; and (c) mineral matter such as gravel, sand, and silt. Compare the amounts, and estimate the percentage composition of each.

   2.   A test for organic matter content is to accurately weigh a thoroughly-dried sample of soil and then burn off the organic matter with a torch. The resulting weight loss is the amount of organic matter that was contained in the sample. Chemical analyses can also be made, but the tests involved are often not practical for school or camp situations. Color is often an indicator of the presence and amount of organic matter—darker soil usually being richer in that respect.

Soil Nutrients or Fertility: 1.   Collect samples of soil from different points and at different levels. Soil from a farm field, a forest topsoil, and a subsoil usually give a good contrast. Place in small flower pots and plant a few bean seeds in each to compare the resulting growth. Fertility is expressed in terms of plant growth with the most growth being from the more fertile soils. Terms that describe fertility are "rank," "healthy," and "sparse."

   2.   Chemical tests can be made for available nitrogen, phosphorus, and potash in soils by using a commercial "soil test" kit; however, growth performance is often a better or more visual test for classroom use.

Water-holding and
Water-absorbing
Capacity:

1. Remove the ends from several tall juice cans, and mark each can 5 centimeters (2 inches) from one end. Place each can upright on the soil to be examined, cover with a board, and drive into the soil to your mark. Pour a liter (1 quart) of water into the can, measuring the distance from the water line to the top of the can each minute for 10 minutes. After 10 minutes, continue measuring at 5-minute intervals until the water has disappeared. Test soils at many locations in this way. The longer it takes for the water to disappear, the less the absorption rate. Does this indicate compaction or texture?

2. Carefully weigh small cans. Place soil samples in them, and carefully weigh them again. Heat in an oven for several hours at a temperature just above boiling. Carefully weigh them again. The percentage of moisture contained in each sample can then be determined.

Erosion and
Slope:

The steeper the slope, the greater the danger of topsoil loss through erosion. Land slope is expressed as a percentage. The *rise* is the vertical distance between the two points, and the *run* is the horizontal distance between the two points. The rise divided by the run then multiplied by 100 gives the percentage of slope.

1. To make a field determination of slope, have the children use a meterstick, place it horizontally, and level it with a carpenter's level. One end must be resting on the soil when checked. Place a second meterstick vertically at right angles to the horizontal stick. The number of centimeters in the second stick is the "percentage of slope."

2. After a heavy rain, collect samples from various slopes and soils, and allow them to stand. Measure the sediment from the various situations, and notice the amount, color, and size of the particles.

3. Splash erosion is the result of the beating of raindrops upon the surface of soil. Splash boards are made from stock about 2 centimeters (1 inch) in

thickness and about 5 centimeters (2 inches) in width. Cut off sections about 45 centimeters (18 inches) in length, and point at one end. Paint the boards white, and mark at 2-centimeter (1-inch) intervals along the entire length. Cut a 20-

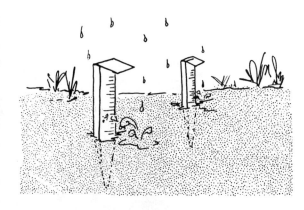

by 15-centimeter (about an 8- by 6-inch) piece of "tin can," and tack length-wise along the square cut end to act as an umbrella or roof.

Place the splash boards at various locations, and read the "splatters" after a rain. Compare the splatters for different kinds of soils and surfaces.

VIII. Interpretive Trails

Interpretive trails, often called "nature trails," have been used in many ways in educational programs. Nearly every interpretive center, whether in a state or national park or in a local forest preserve, has its own "nature trail." Many teachers have used these trails and have adapted and modified the ideas in a variety of ways. One version is known as the "instant trail." Another is known as the "3-meter (10-foot) nature trail," and so on.

The term "interpretive trail" is preferred because it is more inclusive and more appropriately describes the educational use made of this technique. It may also be inappropriate to refer to an interpretive trail that focuses on "metric-concepts," or on concepts such as "smooth" and "flow" as a nature trail.

This section aims to provide readers with a few tips or pointers on the construction and use of interpretive trails. Several abbreviated versions of trail guides used with such interpretive trails are offered to provide an idea of the possibilities. Obviously these guides "fit" a particular site, a particular teaching style, or a particular educational need; hence, they cannot be used by others as they are. Similar activities can be adapted to any location.

The "Permanent" Self-guided Interpretive Trail

Permanent self-guided interpretive trails are often established at outdoor education centers, camps, and interpretive centers. They require a good deal of work to set up properly, and most of them go through a period of being revised and reworked before becoming a reality. Whether the trail one is designing is merely to acquaint users with what is along a given path or whether it is to teach a particular idea or concept matters little, the principles of development are the same.

Such interpretive trails have these elements in common: (1) a series of objects, sites, or stations; (2) a means to inform users how to get from one station to the next in the correct sequence; and (3) an interpretive tool such as a guidebook or tape which provides needed information and which encourages users to perform certain tasks.

Here are some tips that might be useful to readers planning to develop a permanent self-guided interpretive trail:

1. *Clearly define your purposes and objectives.* You may simply have awareness or ecological relationships in mind. You may want to limit it to understandings, or you may want to go beyond this and create interests, skills, and appreciations. Or, you may desire to deal with a single concept such as "green," or "oakiness," or "interaction." Know before beginning what you want to accomplish and stick to it. While it is not uncommon to use the same series of stations for several "interpretive trails," don't plan to do a whole lot of things on one trip.

2. *Study the potential sites—walk the ground.* Identify stations that are appropriate. Make sure that they "mesh" with your objectives, and take advantage of the unique features of your center. For example, an interpretive trail at Norris Geyser Basin in Yellowstone National Park would focus only on the geysers of that basin, not on something else. Be careful that there is the needed degree of permanence in what you have chosen to highlight.

3. *Study the sequence of your stations.* Sometimes things are fixed and you have to go to Station 1 before you go to Station 2 because 2 is further down the path. But, not all interpretive trails are on a trail. Quite often a compass or other means guide users from point to point.

4. *Mark your stations appropriately.* You should use temporary markers at first. After the "kinks" have been worked out, change these to permanent markers. In doing so, attempt to make them sufficient but unobtrusive. They should go unnoticed by those using your route for other purposes. Interpreters in public camps and parks experience great difficulty in keeping such markers in place. Some believe that the only way to have a "permanent" marker is to use a solid steel post set in a large block of concrete.

5. *Decide on your media.* The written word is probably used more frequently than any other media; however, don't go out and get a large number of guides printed immediately. Have a few printed at a time, and revise them for each new printing.

Other approaches are cassette tapes, plug-in earphones and recordings, and a sign at each station with the entire message printed on it.

6. *Establish your message.* Focus in on the message you will try to give. In doing so, stick to your objectives. Include as many "doing" things as possible. There's nothing more dead or uninteresting than an interpretive trail that calls upon the user to walk from station to station to read a few irrelevant facts about each. Have users smell, touch, examine, taste, and measure. They can always be called upon to record, to comment, to describe, and the like. This is especially important for school students.

7. *Develop your message as systematically as possible.* Provide some pertinent information at each station. Offer different experiences to the users by varying the routine from station to station. Require them to record certain data.

8. *Review, evaluate, refine.* Solicit reactions from users; modify accordingly. Spend some time in the background observing users.

9. *Once your interpretive trail is complete, begin to look for additional ways to use it.* Perhaps you will develop a series of guides for the trail applicable to specific user needs. A sixth-grader is quoted as having said that he'd been on a particular "nature trail" in the second grade, the third grade, the fourth grade, and now he was back again in the sixth grade. If nothing else, he should have been provided with different guides and different objectives each year.

Some Ideas for Interpretive Trails

These have been used as the topic or theme for interpretive trails. They might serve as a source of ideas for interpretive trails at your school site or campsite.

1. *The Esti-meter Walk*—focusing on experiences using metric and U.S. units of measure.

2. *The Geology Trail*—focusing on rocks, minerals, landforms, or "time."

3. *Edible Plants*—focusing on things that can be found outdoors and used for food or drink.

4. *Ferns*—focusing on the types of ferns to be found in an area and their specific characteristics.

5. *The Balance Trail*—focusing on a sequence of encounters or experiences designed to improve one's ability to maintain balance.

6. *Tree Identification*—focusing on naming the most common trees found on the school site or campsite.

7. *The Texture Trail*—focusing on the variation in the texture and patterns of the bark of trees.

8. *Historical Places*—focusing on the "artifacts" and relics of the past at the campsite.

9. *The Bird's Nest Trail*—focusing on the examination of the abandoned nests of a variety of birds using the center for nesting purposes.

10. *Trail to Death and Decay*—focusing on the study of the cycle of life.

11. *The Blindfold Trail*—focusing on the "senses" other than "sight." Users are blindfolded and required to use their "other senses" to experience nature.

12. *A Geology Trail Throughout the County*—focusing on stations that are located throughout an entire county or region. Users motor from point to point.

13. *A Historical Trail of the County*—focusing on historical points and sites (similar to No. 12).

14. *Conservation Practices*—focusing on the conservation practices in the county. Users motor from station to station observing the practices without having to leave the public right-of-way.

The Oak Trail

This example is provided to illustrate an approach used to develop the "oak" concept through discussion and observations made at a series of stations in the forest (largely an oak forest) of the Lorado Taft Field Campus. The trees were marked with metal tags, and maps were provided to indicate the location of each station. Similar activities can be adapted to any location.

Objectives: To help students:
1. Identify various oak trees.
2. Appreciate the variety of nature.
3. Develop identification skills.

Equipment: Field glasses.
Rulers.
Paper.
Crayons.
Maps.

Station A. *Trees 1 through 4.* Carefully examine these four trees. Are they the same? Which one is different? Examine the leaves closely to find what the differences are. (The bur oak leaf is large-lobed and wide at the tip.) Measure the length of several leaves from each tree.

Examine the bark of each tree. Notice its texture. Which is rougher? Which has deep grooves and ridges? (Such characteristics are typical of the bur oak.) Do you feel that all oaks will look and feel the same?

Station B. *Tree 5.* There is an oak tree here. Can you find it? (A yellow chestnut or chinquapin sapling.) Look at its leaves. How do they differ from the bur oak leaves? (Leaves are thinner; edges of leaves are saw-toothed.) Can you see the bark? (Probably not.)

How tall is this tree? Estimate its height in meters. In feet. (One way to estimate height is to have a person stand at the base of the tree. Compare his or her height with that of the tree.) Why is it called a sapling? (It is a very young tree.) Look carefully to find any other yellow chestnut oaks in this area. How did this tree get here? Speculate.

Station C. *Trees 6 and 7.* Do you recognize any of these trees? (Tree 6 is a bur oak.) Review the characteristics of the bur oak. Are there any similarities between these and tree 7? (The bark is very similar—deep ridges and very rough.) How are the leaves different? (Black oak leaves are not so wide at the tips; have points on tips; feel thicker and more leathery.) Measure the length of several leaves from this tree. Is this a reliable characteristic? Why? (Leaves vary a great deal in length and shape.) Use the field glasses to examine the upper leaves of this tree.

Station D. *Trees 8 and 9.* Sit down here and examine these trees. Do they appear to be similar to those you've examined before? Notice the color of the bark. Feel the bark. (Seems flaky.) Examine the leaves. (They are similar to the bur oak leaves but not so wide at the tips.) Generally speaking, most oaks have a very characteristic leaf shape that is lobed. Which is the exception? (Yellow chestnut.) Look around you. There are many more white oaks nearby.

Station E. *Trees 10 through 12.* Feel the bark of these three trees. Make rubbings using crayons and paper. Which tree is the white oak? (Tree 10.) What are the other two? (Tree 12 is the same as tree 2 at Station A—a maple. Tree 11 has a very characteristic bark from which it gets its name—shagbark hickory.)

Station F. *Tree 13.* Do you recognize this tree? Examine the leaves. (They are thin and saw-toothed.) This is another yellow chestnut oak. How is this tree different from the first yellow chestnut oak we examined? (It is taller and older, and the bark pattern is more evident.) Are the leaves different? (No.) What can be said about the age of a tree just by examining the leaf? (Very little, although the leaves of a sapling often are larger—thus enabling the tree to absorb more sunlight for growth.)

Station G. *Tree 14.* Examine the bark of this tree and write a description. Describe the leaf. (Bark is grayish, soft, and flaky; leaf is many-lobed, and lobes are rounded and narrower at the tip.) What is this tree? (White oak.) Notice the size of the leaf. Why is it so small? Speculate. (This tree is all alone in the open; it is surrounded by gravel and may not get much water. It may be more than 200 years old.)

Station H. *Tree 15.* Use the field glasses to examine this tree from afar. Notice its characteristics. Come closer, feel the bark, and examine the leaves. Which oak is it? (Black oak.) Can you estimate its age?

Station I. *Tree 16.* Use the field glasses to help you identify this tree. What kind is it? (White oak.) What characteristics helped you make your decision? (White, grayish bark; many lobes on leaves, no points on lobes, thinner leaf tip, etc.)

Station J. *Trees 17 and 18.* Identify these trees. Use the leaves and bark as your clues. (Tree 17 is a black oak, and tree 18 is a white oak.) How tall are these trees? Leaves on these tall trees are too high to reach. They must be examined through the field glasses.

Station K. *Tree 19.* Taking a quick glance, what would you say most of the trees in this forest are? (White oak.) This forest is about 90 percent oak. What is tree 19? Notice the deep ridges in the bark and the pins on the tips of the lobes. (It is a black oak.)

Station L. *Tree 20.* Describe the bark of this tree. Using the field glasses, observe the leaves. You will probably guess that this is a black oak, but it is not. It is a northern red oak. The black oak and red oak are very difficult to tell apart. One characteristic difference is the white streaks in the bark, but that isn't as helpful as it might seem.

Here are some activities you might want to continue in the classroom:

1. Supervise various crafts projects using leaves. Make various kinds of prints.

2. Write stories about trees and our use of them.

3. Whittle or carve oak wood.

4. Find what uses we make of each of the oaks.

The Blindfold Trail

This item is provided to illustrate an approach used to sensitize children to the environment without using the sense of sight. Directions are on a cassette tape, and a rope leads the children from station to station. Similar activities can be adapted to any location.

This trail is designed for the use of children while blindfolded, giving them the opportunity to explore the environment using only their sense of touch. Although sound is incorporated in this trail by the use of oral directions on a tape, the main emphasis is centered around the sense of touch. While it was designed for children at the junior high school level, it can easily be modified for older or younger children and can be set up on almost any school site or other environment.

Objectives: To help students:

1. Develop an awareness of the degree to which they rely on their sense of sight.

2. Take the opportunity to use their sense of touch to gain information about the environment.

3. Develop techniques of problem-solving through individual examination and subsequent group interaction.

Equipment: Tape recorder.
A blindfold for each student.
Rope to be used as a guide from station to station.

Procedure: Divide the students into groups of two to four and blindfold them. Instruct students to keep their right hands on the rope and not to remove their blindfolds. Give the tape recorder to the student in the center of the group. The recorder contains a tape with directions for proceeding on the trail.

Excerpts from the tape follow:

(Start tape.)

You are about to begin the *Eye-Can't-See Trail*. It requires that you use your sense of touch alone to explore the environment. Do not remove your blindfold. As you have been told, the *start* button on the cassette is the one with the masking tape on it. The stop button is the one directly to the left of that. Listen carefully to the directions given on the tape. When you hear the bell, which sounds like this (ring), stop the tape and do as you are told. Sometimes the directions given will only tell you how to get to the next station. Stop the tape while going from station to station. When you get to the station, you will be presented with a problem to solve. Examine the object at the station alone to determine the answer. Do not discuss the answer until you have had an opportunity to find what it is by yourself. Then, discuss the problem as a group, and compare answers. When you have decided what the correct answer is, turn on the tape, and the correct response will be given to you.

You will then be given another problem or the directions to the next station. Do not move away from the marked trail and keep your right hand on the rope while following it. The sound of the bell (ring) indicates when to stop the tape and do as you have been told.

You are now ready to go to the first station. Keep your right hand on the rope, and carefully follow it to the first stake. Find the hard object which is next to the bottom of it. (ring)

Station 1.   What is the object before you on the ground? (ring)

It is a short tree stump. Now, was this tree cut off level or at an angle? (ring)

This tree was cut at an angle. By feeling the edges of the stump, try to tell whether this tree was cut recently or whether it was cut a long time ago? How can you tell? (ring)

It was cut some time ago because the edges have decayed and broken away. You are now ready to go to the second station. Place your right hand on the rope, and walk to the next stake. (ring)

Station 3.   What do you have here? (ring)

It is a wall. Carefully examine it. (ring)

What do you find in the wall? (ring)

There is a window and window sill. How many panes of glass are there in this window? Are they contained in a wood frame? (ring)

85

There are three panes in a metal frame. Now find the stake with the rope attached to it which is found beneath the left side of the window as you face it. Place your right hand on the rope and, counting this stake as number one, carefully walk until you arrive at the fourth stake. (ring)

What is the object that is near to the bottom of this stake? (ring)

Station 6. You have a tree before you with four definite characteristics. Examine the trunk on all sides from the ground up as far as you can reach to determine what these four characteristics are. (ring)

The four characteristics are: (1) very rough bark with ridges, (2) a fuzzy moss growing on the inside cracks of the ridges, (3) two places where branches have been removed and there is no bark, and (4) a growth of woodlike material at the base.

Again, hold the rope in your right hand, and walk carefully until you reach a human-made object. (ring)

Station 9. While holding the branch of the tree in your hand, find a leaf on the branch. Do not remove the leaf, but by touch, try to tell which side of the leaf is the top and which side is the bottom. (ring)

The top is the smooth side—the bottom is less smooth and contains protruding veins. Now examine several leaves to determine whether they are lobed or not and whether the edges are smooth (entire) or toothed. (ring)

The leaves are lobed with smooth edges. These are oak leaves. Again, take the rope in your right hand, and proceed until you reach a human-made object. (ring)

Station 12. Find the corner of this fence. Hold the corner post in your right hand. Proceed to your left along the fence line counting all posts that are embedded in the earth until you reach the next corner. Be careful, there is a gate in the fence. (ring)

There are six posts. If you counted eight, you included the two that are not embedded in the ground. You are to be congratulated, however, because you have successfully made it to the end of the trail. Now, remove your blindfold, return to the first station, and retrace your steps through the trail.

The Esti-meter Walk

This "trail" illustrates the use made of a guide and phenomena found along a forest trail to strengthen metric concepts of distance and interval. The name, "Esti-meter Walk," is very descriptive. Similar activities can be adapted to any location.

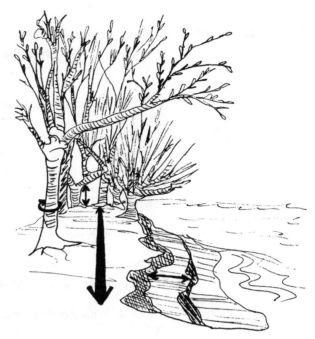

Objectives: To strengthen metric concepts of distances and intervals.

To develop techniques of estimating (judging roughly) sizes and distances in meters and centimeters.

Equipment: A centimeter scale.

A set of answer cards (to be used only after an estimate has been made).

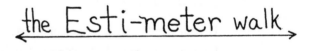

NOTE: A meter consists of 100 centimeters (just as a dollar consists of 100 cents).

Procedure: Have the students assemble near the entrance to the research lab where there are marks on the sidewalk designating length intervals such as 1 meter, 5 meters, 10 meters, etc. Have the students carefully examine and study these distances.

Begin the trail at this point.

This "interpretive trail" follows a total of 18 stations, with the intervals to be estimated and measured increasing in length through the subsequent stations. Trees to be located are identified by arrows.

Samples of six of the stations follow:

Station 1.   Estimate the length of this leaf in centimeters.
   I estimate the length of the leaf to be _____ centimeters.

Check your answer with Answer Card #1.
   What is the actual length of the leaf? _____ centimeters.

If your finger is longer or shorter than the leaf, and if you know the length of the leaf, estimate the length of your finger in centimeters.
   I estimate the length of my finger to be _____ centimeters.

Continue down the trail to Station 2.

Station 2.   There should be a tree stump at your feet. Estimate its diameter in centimeters.
   I estimate the diameter to be _____ centimeters.

Check your answer with Answer Card #2.
   What is the diameter of the tree stump? _____ centimeters.

(Remember, you *do* have a measuring tool with you!)

If your hand span is longer or shorter than the diameter of the tree stump, estimate the length of your hand span in centimeters.
   I estimate the length of my hand span to be _____ centimeters.

Continue down the trail to Station 3.

Station 3.   Locate two trees (identified by arrows). Estimate how many centimeters there are between them. (Remember, you now have two measuring tools!)
   I estimate the distance between the trees to be _____ centimeters.

Check your answer with Answer Card #3.
   What is the correct measurement? _____ centimeters.

If your arm is longer or shorter than the distance between the trees, estimate the length of your arm.
   I estimate the length of my arm (from my elbow to my finger tips) to be _____ centimeters.

Continue down the trail to Station 4.

Station 4. Look at the tree branch above the path. Estimate the distance from the ground to the branch. (Use centimeters and meters for this estimate.)

> I estimate the distance to be _____ centimeters.
>
> I estimate the distance to be _____ meters.

Now, estimate your height in centimeters and meters.

> I estimate my height to be _____ centimeters.
>
> I estimate my height to be _____ meters.

No answer card here! Look under the cup on the path—you will find a measuring line. Use this to check your estimates.

> What is the correct distance between the two trees? _____ centimeters.
> _____ meters.

> What is your correct height? _____ centimeters. _____ meters.

> Continue down the trail to Station 5.

Station 5. This is a starting station. Locate a tree (identified by an arrow). Estimate the distance in centimeters from the Station 5 marker to the tree.

> I estimate the distance to be _____ centimeters.

Check your answer with Answer Card #5.

> What is the correct distance? _____ centimeters.

Continue down the trail to Station 6. Watch the path carefully.

Station 6. Locate two trees (identified by arrows). Estimate the distance between the trees in centimeters. (Remember your measuring tools!)

> I estimate the distance between the two trees to be _____ centimeters.

Using your arm span, measure the distance.

> The distance is _____ centimeters.

Check your answers with Answer Card #6.

> What is the distance between the trees? _____ centimeters.

Continue down the trail to Station 7. Watch your step carefully because you are going across a gully.

JO-EL-IE Ecology Trail

We have learned that all life is intimately connected with other life in a chain of relationships beginning with the sun. A careful examination of links in that chain reveals "Nature's Plan of Survival."

JO-EL-IE Ecology Trail begins at the west side of Browne House. Look for the marker.

Station 1.   *Kentucky Coffee Trees.* Notice the two mature Kentucky coffee trees and the two younger ones struggling for survival under the dominance of the oaks and the building. Kentucky coffee trees have leaves up to nearly a meter (3 feet) in length with as many as 100 leaflets.

Station 2.   *Top of Observation Tower.* Look around you. What kinds of trees are the tallest? What caused the death of some of the trees? Notice the vine climbing the locust tree. Trees are called "friends of the earth." Their overhead canopy provides shade from the sun, softens the fall of rain, and adds moisture and oxygen to the air. Later, their decaying leaves, trunks, and roots make the soil fertile. Many animals live in the woods: worms, insects, and moles in the soil; squirrels, owls, and woodpeckers in the hollow trees; birds in the tree branches; foxes, chipmunks, and rabbits in underground burrows—all of these animals find food and shelter in the woods. Many of them assist the trees by eating insects, improving soil, and spreading seeds. Each plant or animal "benefits" the community in which it lives. On your way to the prairie look for *mole runs.*

Station 3. *The Prairie.* Look right! Look left! Look behind you! The *invaders* are coming! The *quaking aspens* are moving in! From the periphery of the prairie, the aspens move in by suckering, and the oaks and elms move in by seeding. Why do we even have this "break" in the tree line? Why hasn't it been taken over by the aspen and other growth?

Prairie plants can withstand the dryness and heat of summer and the winds and cold of winter. They manage with little water. Many plants and animals of the prairie would perish if transplanted to a forest or marsh for they would no longer have the conditions of temperature and moisture to which they are adapted.

Station 4. *Fungi.* Fungi grow everywhere. Fungi help to enrich soil by causing decay in living and dead plants. Mushrooms and toadstools are familiar fungi. Fungi are indispensable to the healthy functioning of a woodland: they provide food for the insects, turtles, small mammals, slugs, and snails; they help to break down woody tissue.

Station 5. *Twisty Tree.* Why has this been named "Twisty Tree"? What has caused it to twist and turn so? Vines are plants that do not support themselves. Once a vine is able to grow above its support, it may shade the trees below. Vines tend to maintain clearings in the woods because they retard the growth of new trees. Vines produce fruits upon which many birds and mammals feed.

Station 6. *Wild Grape.* Some 26 kinds of birds eat wild grapes. The red-eyed vireo, a small bird, uses strips of the bark in its nest while the vine itself often supports many nests. Foxes, skunks, opossums, and rabbits also eat the fruit.

Station 7. *Pouch Galls.* The most intriguing thing about galls is that they are growths induced by agents external to the plant, the wild plum. The plant actually grows a type of new organ which nurtures and shelters young insects. The mites which produce these reddish pouch galls are individually smaller than the head of a pin. Notice what is happening to the leaves of the plum tree.

Station 8. *Plant Succession.* This grassland area may someday be a forest. Under the soil are earthworms and numerous minute animals, plants, and roots. These burrow in the soil and loosen, aerate, and make it fertile. The fertile, young, sun-loving trees that are beginning to grow will soon kill the grass. Eventually forest trees will invade the area. Human presence is also evident. Are we also a part of nature's community?

Station 9. *Exposed Root System.* Notice the erosion of the soil at your feet. Did humans play a part in this "destruction"? Look to your left. The depth of soil on most of the earth's surface is no more than a few centimeters (inches). The damage done in many areas by soil erosion may require millenniums to erase.

Station 10. *Eastern Red Cedars.* These trees are partial to limestone soils and often grow where the soil is quite barren. Besides providing excellent food and cover for wild birds, they are also used by humans for making many things.

Station 11. *Fallen Leaves.* Leaves return minerals to the soil when they fall. These leaves become humus which enables the soil to retain water, thus preventing heavy rains from carrying the soil away.

Station 12. *Eagle's Nest Tree.* What caused the odd shape of this tree? Is it shaped the same as the others we passed? Trees growing in exposed areas, particularly on mountain tops or cliffs, develop this shape. Why?

SUMMARY: As you walked along the trail you saw how the earth's most important resources are dependent upon each other. Not one of the four—soil, water, plants, animals—goes unchanged by the others.

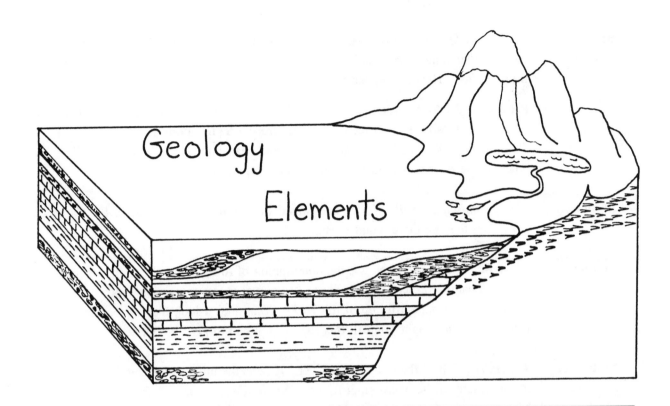

Geology

Elements

This *Geology Trail Guide* is provided only as a sample. It is a question guide. When used with an accompanying answer guide, it can be self-teaching. Leaders working with children find guides of this type helpful. Each child should have a question guide; whereas, only the leader or teacher may have access to the answer guide. Similar activities can be adapted to any location.

Equipment: Rock hammers.   Safety goggles.
              Dilute HCl.   Thermometers.
              Knives.   Rock and fossil guide books.
              Hand lenses.   Specimen collecting bags.

Station 1.   *The Tower.* Take a good look at the river valley below. What are the geological and topographical features that catch your eye? On what types of a formation is the camp located? Can you see "David's Tower"? Can you tell where the plain was at one time? What do you call the flat region on the far side of the river? Can you see a "basin" or an "escarpment"? How are they formed?

Station 2.   *The Quarry.* Notice the cracks that run horizontally and vertically through this bedrock. How do you suppose they happened? More about these joints at the next station.

Station 3.   *Ganymedes Spring.* Do you know a legend about Ganymedes? It has a connection with another famous landmark in this area. Where does the spring water come from? Why? How? Why isn't the water fit to drink?

Place a hand into the water, and estimate the temperature of the water. After all of your guesses have been recorded, measure the temperature accurately with a thermometer. Will this temperature vary from season to season? Will it vary as much as the river temperature? Proceed along the trail.

Station 4.   *Along Sinnissippi Trail.* Notice the "wash" on the bluff to the right of the trail. How does the tree there retard erosion?

Station 5.   *Along Sinnissippi Trail.* Notice the outcropping of rocks above the trail. Do you know its name? Proceed along the trail just a few feet to another type of rock outcropping. Scrape off a bit of this rock. What does it look like? What does it feel like? What might you call this rock if you had to give it a name?

Station 6.   *The Gully.* Follow the gully to the river. How is the mouth of this gully similar to the mouth of the Mississippi River? Where did the material from which the "delta" is composed originate? How was this material carried here? Why was it deposited here? Trace the gully upstream.

Station 7.   *In the Gully.* What is the difference between the two banks of the gully? What would cause the difference? Can you see a place where the stream bed might have been in the past? What indicates that a creek or river is a poor land boundary?

Station 8.   *In the Gully.* Notice the trees and how they hold the soil in place. What happened to the soil that once covered their exposed roots? How have the roots changed since they were uncovered? Why did the roots turn in? Take a sample of this soil back to the laboratory to test to see if it is "sour" or "sweet." A thought question: Why does a dry stream bed make an excellent place for rock collecting?

Station 9.   *In the Gully.* Many rocks found here are "foreigners." Why? See how many of these "foreign" rocks you can find. Bring samples with you to classify and identify in the laboratory.

Station 10.   *Right Side of the Gully.* Compare the soil profile diagram with the cross section of soil found in the bank of this gully. What might have caused these alternate layers of rock and soil? Can you piece together a story after some observation? Might these alternate layers of topsoil, clay, rock, clay, soil, and rock be compared to the growth rings of a tree?

Station 11. *Still in the Gully.* From this point notice the other branches of the drainage system. Sketch a map showing this drainage pattern. What type of drainage pattern is this? Observe the broad valley of the gully and the winding course the stream bed follows. What are the big curves called? As you move along and follow the right-hand branch of the gully, look for old stream beds.

Station 12. *In the Gully.* Can you find where the stream once flowed? What is this "type" of landform called? How does it form?

Station 13. *"C" Trail.* Observe another type of soil-building process at this point. Can you see here the importance of decaying logs, leaves, bacteria, and fungi in the balance of nature? Is there anything in the world that is ALL bad or ALL good? Is there any value in death? Explain!

Station 14. *"C" Trail.* From this point we have an overall view of the gully. Notice how it winds around and meanders. Notice how the general direction it flows changes at the foot of the backbone. Return to the laboratory to identify your samples of rocks.

NOTE: A geology trail which is valid one year may not be so the next year. In certain areas, erosion may have completely changed station views of the region. You should always "preview" the trail before you have your students use it.

IX. Magnetic Compasses

Children of almost any age or grade level can learn how to use magnetic compasses. Your children may gain insights into direction and magnetism merely by handling these instruments. Older children will find them useful in getting from "where they are to where they want to be" or in measuring angles. In doing so, they will develop understanding about navigation, maps, mapping, and geometric figures.

The importance of magnetic compasses in the exploration of the western world should not be underestimated and should be understood by compass users. The origin of the compass itself is not clear (see appropriate encyclopedia articles) and is a good example to illustrate that many of our understandings of history are vague and incomplete.

The ideas and activities included in this section have been used successfully with children and illustrate ways to help them to understand and use compasses and the ways that compasses may be used to provide learning experiences on school sites and at camp settings—experiences in which children are directly involved.

Ideally, each youngster should be furnished with a compass while completing one of these activities. Certainly, no more than three children should have to share one compass. The cost of a compass varies with the type and quality wanted. The Silva, or "scout" compass, costs around $5 to $10 each. Better Silva compasses may be obtained from any one of a number of suppliers of school and camp equipment for around $15 each. Many teachers prefer the Silva because it has a plastic base and a "direction of travel" arrow. Other types without this feature are available and suitable for many of these experiences and are actually preferred by other teachers.

Additional information and suggestions concerning the use of compasses may be obtained from Kjellstrom's *Be Expert with Map and Compass: The Orienteering Handbook.*

Using a Silva Compass

Parts:

Plastic base
    Direction of travel arrow
    Scale (inches and millimeters)
Metal or plastic housing
    Red-tipped magnetic needle (the red tip always
    points toward the north magnetic pole unless
    another magnetic influence is nearby)
Black- or red-outlined arrow
    (orienting arrow)
Numerical degrees (0 to 360 degrees)
Letter directions (N, E, S, W)

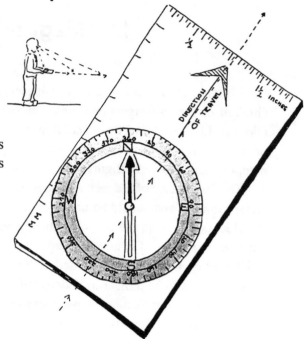

How to Use the Silva Compass

Following a Trail

1. Decide the direction that you wish to go in numerical degrees (azimuth or letter direction).

2. Hold the *plastic base* and turn the *housing* so as to align the desired azimuth or direction reading with the *direction of travel arrow* on the base.

3. With the *direction of travel arrow* pointing in the direction you are facing, turn your body, holding the compass level and close in front of you, until the *red-tipped needle* and the *outlined arrow* (orienting arrow) point the same way. You should now be facing in the direction you want to go.

4. Sight over the *direction of travel arrow* into the distance to some object. Walk the given distance toward that object.

Constructing a Trail

1. Hold the compass level. Point the *direction of travel arrow* at the object to which you wish to know the direction (degree or azimuth) reading.

2. Turn the *housing* until the *red-tipped needle* and the *black-outlined arrow* (orienting arrow) are aligned and point the same way.

3. Read the azimuth (on the *housing)* above the *direction of travel arrow.* This is the direction that you must travel to get to that point.

   NOTE: Notice the compass in the above sketch. It is set to travel in a northeasterly direction at an azimuth of 40 degrees.

Geometric Figures with a Magnetic Compass

Objectives: To provide experience with a magnetic compass.
To improve concepts of simple geometric figures.

Equipment: A compass.
Six or seven colored flags or markers for each child or pair of children.
An open area or field.

Preparation: Provide indoor instruction about geometric figures, angles, degrees, and the use of a compass. This exercise provides experience following such instruction. It helps if markers of several colors are used—all those used by a particular child or pair of children being the same color.

Procedure: Position children (leaving several steps between each child). Do not inform them of the types of figures they will be constructing.

Constructing a Square

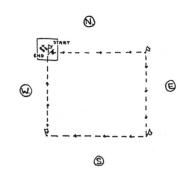

1. Place first marker at feet.
2. Walk 10 steps at an azimuth of 90 degrees and place the second marker.
3. Walk 10 steps at 180 degrees and place the third marker.
4. Walk 10 steps at 270 degrees and place the fourth marker.
5. Walk 10 steps at 360 degrees and place the fifth marker.

Now step back to look at the area each has enclosed. Measure the distance between the first and fifth markers. (Markers 1 and 5 should be at the same place.) What type of figure should have resulted? Review the directions, discuss errors, and analyze figures as to length of sides, angles, etc.

Constructing an Equilateral Triangle

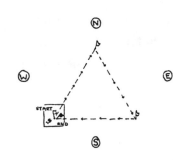

1. Place first marker at feet.
2. Walk 10 steps at an azimuth of 30 degrees and place the second marker.
3. Walk 10 steps at 150 degrees and place the third marker.
4. Walk 10 steps at 270 degrees and place the fourth marker.

Measure the interval between the first and fourth markers. (Markers 1 and 4 should be at the same place.) Why use a difference of 120 degrees between each of the three azimuths when there are only 60 degrees in each of the angles of the triangle? Review the directions, discuss errors, and analyze figures as to length of sides, angles, etc.

Constructing a Trapezoid

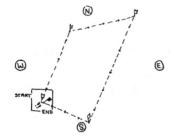

1. Place first marker at feet.
2. Walk 10 steps at an azimuth of 30 degrees and place the second marker.
3. Walk 10 steps at 75 degrees and place the third marker.
4. Walk 17 steps at 210 degrees and place the fourth marker.
5. Walk 7 steps at 300 degrees and place the fifth marker.

(Markers 1 and 5 should be at the same place.) Review the directions, discuss errors, and analyze figures as to length of sides, angles, etc.

Constructing a Hexagon

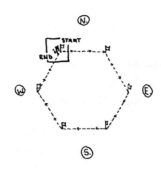

1. Place first marker at feet.
2. Walk 10 steps at an azimuth of 90 degrees and place the second marker.
3. Walk 10 steps at 150 degrees and place the third marker.
4. Walk 10 steps at 210 degrees and place the fourth marker.
5. Walk 10 steps at 270 degrees and place the fifth marker.
6. Walk 10 steps at 330 degrees and place the sixth marker.
7. Walk 10 steps at 30 degrees and place the seventh marker.

(Markers 1 and 7 should be at the same place.) Review the directions, discuss errors, and analyze figures as to length of sides, angles, etc.

Follow-up Indoors: Construct these same figures to scale on paper. Use protractors instead of magnetic compasses using the same directions given for outdoors. Orient properly with a north-south line on the paper. (Is this a map-making activity?)

Construction of Geometric Figures with a Magnetic Compass

Objectives: To apply and improve compass skills.

To clarify concepts of distance, direction, geometric figures, perimeter, area, and other geometric relationships.

Equipment: (for each team of three or four students)

Six stakes (labeled A, B, C, D, E, F).

One or more magnetic compasses.

A ball of string.

An open area or field.

Preparation: Students should be familiar with the compass and know how to use it. They should be able to measure sizes of angles, to lay out angles of given sizes, and to determine the length of their own step or pace.

Constructions

The Square. Place Stake A at a convenient point, and let it be the NW corner of the square. Make a 20-step line directly SOUTH from this point (this becomes your WEST boundary). Drive Stake B at the SW corner, Stake C at the SE corner, and Stake D at the NE corner, forming a square 20 steps on each side.

Angle Bisectors. With your magnetic compass, bisect the angle at each of the four corners.

Do your bisectors intersect at one point? _____ Should they? _____

If they do, drive Stake E at this point.

Bisector of Side BA. Drive Stake F on the mid point of Side BA. This point should be

WEST of Stake E. Is it? _____

Fencing (optional). Connect all points possible using strings (omit strings between F and C and between F and D).

Measurements: You lack standard measures and units to find the distance between points in your construction; hence, decide on some item as a standard unit (suggestion: step, length of convenient stick, etc.). What did you select?

_____

1. With your unit, measure the distance between these points:

   A – C _____   F – A _____   E – B _____

   A – B _____   E – F _____   E – D _____

   C – D _____   B – D _____   F – B _____

   E – A _____   B – C _____

   E – C _____   D – C _____

2. Count the similar angles in your construction. How many are right angles (90 degrees)?

   _____ 45 degrees angles? _____

3. Since you have measured the distance between each pair of stakes and the angles of the triangles in your construction, you can answer these questions about the areas and perimeters:

   a. What is the area in your units of the square ABCD? _____

   b. Compare the sum of the areas of the triangles ABC and BDC with the area of the square ABCD. What is the ratio? _____

   c. Compare the area of triangle AED or CED with the area of the square ABCD. What is the ratio? _____

   d. What is the perimeter of ABCD? _____ ABC? _____

   AED? _____ AEF? _____

4. Similar and congruent triangles:

   a. Locate four triangles that are alike (congruent). They are: _____,

   _____, _____, and _____.

   b. Indicate at least three pairs of congruent triangles: _____ and _____.

   _____ and _____. _____ and _____.

   c. How many isosceles triangles (having two equal sides and angles) can you find?

   _____

5. Locate two trapezoids. How many sides and corners does each have?_____

   _____

6. What generalizations can you draw about the bisectors of the angles of a square (by examining your construction)?

    a. _____

    b. _____

    c. _____

7. What is the direction (in degrees) from:

    A to B? _____   C to A? _____   E to F? _____

    B to A? _____   A to C? _____   F to E? _____

SUMMARY: Discuss with the other members of your team the relationships you have seen, some of the ideas you have developed, and the advantages and disadvantages of approaching this problem in this way as compared to construction with a pencil and paper in the classroom.

Constructing a Teaching Compass Course

Teaching compass courses may be used nearly anyplace (school sites, campsites, etc.) to help develop children's concepts and understandings. They are really interpretive trails using compass directions to get users from point to point. Their features include:

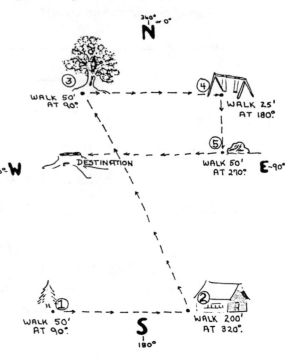

1. Teaching stations and/or locations.

2. Comments, questions, and activities at each station on what the learner is to observe, measure, do, or accomplish.

3. Directions leading learners from station to station.

A teaching compass course has many purposes:

1. To apply and develop compass skills.

2. To orient students to an area or to serve as an awareness experience.

3. To provide identification experiences (trees, rocks, buildings, etc.).

4. To develop a concept (ecology, geology, similarities and differences, green, etc.).

5. To focus attention on individual specimens or situations.

A good compass course requires much work and time to construct or set up; hence, several leaders may wish to plan and develop the activity jointly. They must:

1. Clearly define the educational purposes and objectives.

2. Select the stations and develop activities, data gathering, observations, and questions applicable to each. (Refer to the section on interpretive trails.)

3. Determine the sequence of the stations in the compass course.

4. Develop directions to lead students from station to station:

   a. Measure the distances accurately (children may pace these distances).

b. Determine the azimuths from station to station. (Check and recheck.)

c. Provide hints to tell children if they are near to where they should be. (Examples: "There should be a chimney to your right." "A large oak tree stands just to the west.")

5. Design a course to provide the students with directions for completing the entire course at the beginning, or design one to require the students to discover the directions as they proceed from station to station.

6. Prepare the students beforehand. The students may work individually or in small groups. They should:

a. Know the reason for the compass course.

b. Know their step length.

c. Know how to convert meters or yards to steps. (Here is an application of ratio and proportion.)

d. Know how to use a magnetic compass.

e. Have pencils, paper, compasses, and other apparatus.

7. Follow up indoors. After returning to the classroom, review the compass course. Deal with the comments and activities at each station. Perhaps some students will wish to construct a map of the route followed in the compass course. Perhaps the students will want to develop a compass course for others to experience.

A Sample Compass Course

This sample illustrates one type of teaching compass course. It provides students with experiences using the magnetic compass and orients them to the buildings area of the Lorado Taft Field Campus of Northern Illinois University. A similar activity can be adapted to any location.

Once students have been taught the use of the compass and a way to measure distance intervals by pacing, they are taken to the starting point and given a card like that shown below. If they follow the directions, and if "all goes well," they are led to a second card. It contains directions to the third card, and so on, through a sequence of five or six cards. Students are required to do assignments at each station.

As a result of completing this course, students will understand the use of a magnetic compass and have completed enough experiences and activities to give them a good idea of the facilities and what is available. It is very useful to have several courses like this (all beginning from the same location) so that each team of three or four students will have a different route.

COMPASS ORIENTATION COURSE A　　　Team Members _____
　　　Card 1　　　　　　　　　　　　　　　　_____
　　　　　　　　　　　　　　　　　　　　　　_____

Follow directions carefully.
Answer all questions.

1.　Leave Poley House through the east door, and step to the tray. Walk 54 meters (59 yards) at an azimuth of 156 degrees. What human-made structure do you see immediately to the west? _____ Why might someone build something like this here? Is there some local history about this that we might want to explore? Where and how can we find out? _____
　　_____
　　_____

2.　Walk 82 meters (268 feet) at an azimuth of 100 degrees. You should now be at the corner of a residence. Next, go 53 meters (175 feet) at an azimuth of 30 degrees, and stand on human-made stone. Next, take 12 steps at an azimuth of 84 degrees. Enter the room nearest to you. What would you assume to be the purpose of this room?
　　_____
　　_____

　　If there is an envelope labeled for Group A, open it and follow the directions. Do not disturb any envelopes not intended for your team.

Fifteen Degrees

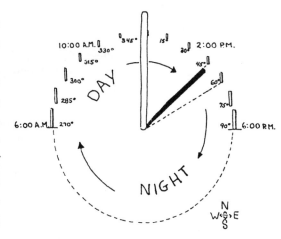

This concept ties together (1) the magnetic compass, (2) a timepiece, (3) astronomy, (4) the sextant, (5) the sundial, and (6) the calendar.

Many kinds of activities can stem from the earth's rotation, thereby creating a thread that runs through astronomy, compass work, and time. These activities lead to an understanding of the calendar and help us to understand the apparent movement of the stars, planets, and moon. Students can then make sundials, understand the sextant, use a compass to estimate time, and even use a watch to find directions.

Basic Idea: The earth revolves around the sun approximately once every 365 days. The earth rotates on its inclined (23½ degrees) axis once every 24 hours. Since there are 360 degrees in a circle, the earth rotates about 15 degrees each hour.

Activities and Questions:

1. Place stakes or markers around a tall central point such as a flagpole or other tall post; one stake at the end of the post's shadow for each hour of the day and/or one stake for each 15 degrees away from North.

    a. Make compass readings of the direction of the shadow (caused by the sun) corresponding to the stakes set for each hour of the day (sunrise to sunset) or at other time intervals.

    b. Make hourly readings of time for each 15-degree stake, dawn to dusk.

    c. Select compass readings (such as 300 degrees, 330 degrees, 30 degrees, etc.), and determine the time of day when the shadow falls in these directions.

2. Questions similar to these may be helpful in observing, recording, and analyzing data:

    a. Through how many degrees does the earth rotate in one hour? How can you demonstrate this?

    b. How do the daylight hours for winter and summer compare? (Actual observer data can be compared to that taken from references.) Measure the period of daylight each month.

c. How can a watch be used as a compass? One method is to point the hour hand at the sun. Bisect the angle between the hour hand and 12. That should be south. Check the *standard* time. Why?

d. Diagram the apparent motion of the sun and determine if the earth rotates in a clockwise or a counterclockwise manner. Which way do we spin?

e. Why do the sun, the planets, the stars, and the moon appear to move around the earth?

f. Observe the night sky at various times throughout a night. What star does not appear to move? (Polaris) Why is this the case? Is this useful? Plot the course of the Big Dipper around Polaris (North Star).

g. What is a "winter sky" or "summer sky"? Have children observe the sky at 8:00 P.M., 5:00 A.M., and at other times on a given night. Must we wait until winter to see a winter sky?

h. In what way does the path of a planet differ from that of a star? Continue your observations over a period of several weeks.

i. If you were to fix a time-lapse camera on Polaris for about two hours, what would your picture look like? Make a drawing.

j. Investigate to learn how a sextant works. Could you use a clinometer or make one from a ruler, protractor, piece of string, and sighting level to mark and predict the movement of stars around Polaris?

k. Can you make a sundial? Why not do it?

l. A real challenge. Through direct observation and measurement, determine "where on earth you are." Hint: What do the terms "longitude" and "latitude" really mean?

"Orienteering"

"Orienteering" is a very popular sport. A contestant has a map on which the locations of several post or checkpoints are marked. The contestant who gets to these checkpoints in the shortest period of time is the winner.

An adaptation which is often rated by students (upper elementary through graduate school) as a highlight of a multiday outdoor education experience is described below.

Equipment: 1.   Multiple copies of a map of the area (a reproduction of a Soil Conservation Service [SCS] aerial photograph will do).

                  2.   A number of distinctly-marked posts or markers set at appropriate locations (each marked with a different set of colors). Two of these should be located about 100 meters (70 yards) from each other to use as starting locations. (With 2 starting posts and 7 additional markers in the field, one can handle 14 teams of 2, 3, or 4 students at once.) Each team should have its own unique route to follow to three or four of the checkpoints and to the finish point.

Preparation: Preliminary instruction requires at least an hour. It should deal with:

                  1.   The magnetic compass, its origin, operation, use, application, and limitations.

                  2.   Measurement of distances in the field. If your map has a scale of 1 : 10,000, the student might pace a distance of 100 meters (70 yards). In doing so, the student has the number of steps needed to cover the distance represented by one centimeter (.4 inch) on the map. Why?

                  3.   Orienting a map or turning it so that the North–South indicator lies parallel with the poles of the earth. (Depending upon the location, allowance or correction must be made for "declination"—the compass needle being attracted toward the north magnetic pole instead of the true North Pole.)

                  4.   Orienting and setting the compass to follow the assigned route. Before a team is given the map marked with the route it will use, it should complete a practice exercise in setting the compass, finding the azimuth to one or two points, measuring the interval to be traveled, and calculating the number of steps to get there. Check these carefully.

Observations: Various data-gathering experiences can be completed enroute to the checkpoints (i.e., students might pretend that they are explorers, like Lewis and Clark, and are gathering information to send back to "civilization"; or they might be required to list the trees, birds, or signs of people that they encounter).

Proof that they have reached their checkpoints is their record of the correct color combinations on the checkpoints.

CAUTION: Use prudence in deciding how much freedom to give a team of students in going from point to point. Be in the field to check up. An aide or counselor might accompany groups of younger children. Modify the course as appropriate for the terrain. This has even been successfully accomplished on an open, closely mowed field, with the checkpoints being laid flat on the ground and all groups being visible to the instructor at all times.

X. Measurement and Mapping

Although some understanding of measurement can be achieved in classrooms, real understanding may not be obtained until first-hand field experiences are provided with large-scale measurement and map construction.

Teachers know that it is easy to construct right angles or to "lay out" *a square* on paper, but constructing similar figures (such as a baseball diamond) in the field is a different matter—and a challenge for most children.

There is also some doubt about the accuracy of children's percepts or mental images of intervals and quantities (such as distance, height, weight, volume, etc.) unless they have had some direct field experiences. Although children use phrases such as (1) an acre of land, (2) a hundred-foot tree, (3) a distance of one-half kilometer, etc., their mental picture of the interval or quantity is likely to be vague. To test the mental images (concepts) held by your students, ask each one to (1) lift a rock or block of wood and record an estimate of its weight, (2) estimate the distance between two buildings, (3) estimate the temperature in Celsius degrees, and (4) estimate the quantity of water in a puddle, etc. You will be surprised by the range and variation in the replies of a typical class of students.

The following activities are illustrative of the types of experiences that can and should be provided on school sites and in camp settings. Obviously, they will be modified in approach and complexity to fit the children, the field resources available, the curricula, and the interest and competencies of the leaders.

Estimating Experiences Using U.S. and Metric Units

Although the *metric system* is the international standard of measure, relatively few people in the United States appear to understand the relationship between it and our traditional measurement units. Experiences listed below are designed to help individuals develop some understanding of metric units and traditional units through "estimating experiences" indoors and outdoors.

Directions: Have a pair of students work together on each item so they can discuss the problem and arrive at a tentative conclusion which can be verified later through actual measurement using appropriate instruments.

Estimates

Indoors

1. Height of table:

    _____ inches _____ centimeters

2. Height of ceiling:

    _____ inches _____ centimeters

3. Size of room:

    _____ sq. feet _____ sq. meters

4. Circumference of globe:

    _____ inches _____ centimeters

5. Length of hallway:

    _____ feet _____ meters

6. Volume of wastebasket:

    _____ gallons _____ liters

7. Weight of wooden block:

    _____ pounds _____ kilograms

8. Weight of rock:

    _____ pounds _____ kilograms

Outdoors

1. Length of one side of school building:

    _____ feet _____ meters

2. Distance between the bottom of a window in the school to the ground:

    _____ feet _____ meters

3. Area of land enclosed within four stakes:

    _____ acres _____ hectares

4. Height of the flagpole:

    _____ feet _____ meters

5. Height of the chimney:

    _____ feet _____ meters

6. Outdoor air temperature:

    _____ Fahrenheit _____ Celsius

7. Weight of a second rock:

    _____ pounds _____ kilograms

After all students have had an opportunity to make their estimates, measure the intervals and quantities. Compare the estimates with the actual measurements. *Repeat the activity regularly using different intervals and quantities.* Keep a record of how accurately students estimate!

NOTE: This activity is much more effective if the students estimate, record their estimate, and then measure the interval in sequence.

Developing Distance Percepts—The 30-Meter Exercise

Objectives: To improve percepts of distance and clarify measurement concepts. (If not working with metric units, an interval of 100 feet or any other convenient interval can be used instead of 30 meters.)

Equipment: Four flags or markers (white, black, red, green) per student.
These can be made by tying a strip of colored cloth onto the looped end of a stiff wire (coat hanger).
Several metersticks.
Several measuring tapes.
Ball of twine.

Preparation: In an open field, place a marker in position and attach the twine, extending it in a convenient direction for about 75 meters.

Activity

1. *Sight Guessing.* Beginning at the reference marker, have the students back away from it along the twine and place their white flag at the point they guess to be 30 meters from the reference marker. Caution the students to use their own judgment and to keep track of their own flag. When all markers are in place, step away to note the *range* of guesses, clusters of flags (modes), etc. Locate the median. Leave all flags in place.

2. *Pacing.* Have the students repeat the process using a part of their body (length of foot, length of arm, length of step, etc.) to help make their estimate. Have them mark this estimate of 30 meters with their black flag. The range of estimates will probably narrow on this attempt. The students should have a better idea of the interval than at the first guess.

3. *Measuring with a Meterstick.* Next, instruct the students to measure the distance interval with a meterstick and to mark this measurement with their red flag. The range should narrow to only a few centimeters on this trial. Students will now want to know who was "closest." Explain that they used three approaches, that there is still a range, and that you still don't know exactly where the 30-meter point lies. How will you ever know?

4. *Measuring with a Measuring Tape.* Assign a few pairs of students to carefully measure the 30 meters using measuring tapes and marking the point with their green flag. Even now, a range of a fraction of a centimeter will be evident. Discuss the possible reasons for this.

Analysis and Follow-up:

Older students may develop frequency distributions and polygons of the estimates and compute other statistics. They will then know if the class overestimated or underestimated, if boys did better than girls, etc.

The exercise may occasionally be repeated using various intervals. Always compare with earlier attempts to see if there is any improvement.

Provide additional practice in estimating and measuring different intervals both indoors and outdoors.

Area, Perimeter, and Average

Through outdoor experiences, the mathematical percepts of area, perimeter, and average can be clarified, modified, or reinforced through problem situations. The following are illustrative of activities which can take place on the school site or campsite.

1. Using four stakes, each marking a corner of the plot, lay out or mark out a designated plot of ground which contains a variety of trees.

    a. Using a meterstick (yardstick), measure the distance between Stakes 1 and 2; 2 and 3; 3 and 4; and 4 and 1. Add all four distances. This answer can be designated as "perimeter."

    b. Calculate the number of square meters (square feet) contained within the four stakes.

    c. Using any form of indirect measurement, ascertain the height of each tree within the plot of ground. Arrive mathematically at an average for the height of all the trees.

    d. Measure the diameter of each tree about a meter (3 feet) above the ground. Determine the range of difference in diameter, and calculate the average diameter of the trees.

2. Using a string of at least 30 meters (100 feet) in length as a radius, mark out a large circle.

    a. Carefully measure the diameter of this circle. Carefully measure the circumference. Divide the circumference by the diameter. The answer you get should be about *3.14.*

    b. Repeat the above, using circles of different diameters. What generalization appears?

    c. Calculate the area—in square meters (square feet)—of your largest circle. Divide this by the circumference (perimeter). Which shape gives you the most area per unit of perimeter, the rectangle or the circle?

Four Ways to Estimate Heights

Shadow–Ratio Method

Place a stick of known length (meterstick) perpendicular to the ground, and measure its shadow.

Measure the length of the shadow cast by the object being measured.

Use this proportion:

$$\frac{\text{Shadow of Object}}{\text{Shadow of Stick}} = \frac{\text{Height of Object}}{\text{Height of Stick}}$$

Example: Meterstick casts shadow of 0.66 meter. Tree casts 10-meter shadow

$$\frac{10}{0.66} = \frac{\text{Tree Height}}{1}$$

Tree Height = 15 meters

9:1 Ratio or Similar Triangles

Measure nine paces from the base of the object (tree), and push a meterstick into the ground at that point.

Continue one pace farther, and mark it. Lie on the ground at this point, and, sighting with your eye, project a line past the stick to the top of the tree.

The height on the stick in centimeters where the projected line of sight passed is the height of the tree in decimeters.

Explain!

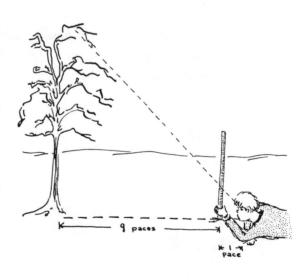

116

Artist's Method

Have a person whose height you know stand by the object to be measured. Use this person as your "unit of measurement."

Hold a stick (or pencil) at arm's length. Sight over the top of the stick to the head of the "unit of measurement." Place your thumbnail on the stick where the line of sight meets the person's foot.

Determine the number of times the "unit of measurement" fits onto the object being measured by moving the stick upwards a unit at a time.

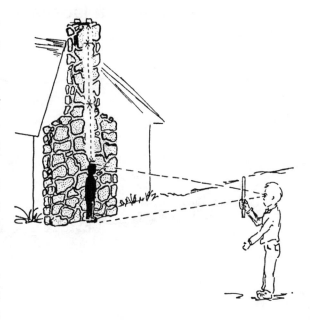

NOTE: A similar method, called the totem-pole method, is used to establish elevation concepts. A child moves down the hill until his or her eyes are at ground level with the starting point. A second child moves farther down the slope until his or her eyes are level with the feet of the first child. Continue until each child has been placed or the distance has been covered. Count the number of "units" (children) to obtain the depth.

Isosceles Right-Triangle Method

Back away from the object (tree) until an imaginary line from your eye to the top of tree forms a 45-degree angle to a *horizontal* line from your eye to the tree. Use a clinometer (vertical protractor) to help find the correct angle.

In a 45-degree right triangle (isosceles right triangle), the two sides are equal in length; hence, distance "A" is equal to distance "B" (figure at right).

To find the height of the object, measure the distance from you to the object, and add this amount to the height of your eyes from ground level.

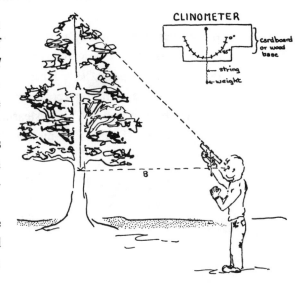

117

Measuring the Width of a River Using a Magnetic Compass and an Isosceles Right Triangle

Select a clearly visible point "A" across the river.

Mark your position "B" with a stake or post and walk along the river's edge until you reach point "C" at which a line from there to point "A" on the other side makes a 45-degree angle with the line back to "B." (Use the magnetic compass to measure the 45-degree angle.)

In a 45-degree (isosceles) right triangle, the two sides of the triangle are equal in length. (In the above illustration, distance "D" equals distance "E.") To learn the approximate width of the river, therefore, measure distance "D" between points "B" and "C."

Example: If the river flows directly north or south and you are on the east shore, points "A" and "C" should be selected with a compass so that point "A" is 270 degrees (azimuth) from point "B." Then point "C" should be established by going south along the shore until you get a compass reading of 315 degrees (270 degrees + 45 degrees) from it to point "A." Measure distance "D" either by using a tape measure or by pacing. If this is 50 meters (164 feet), then the river is approximately 50 meters (164 feet) in width.

A Sighting Board to Help Estimate Distances

An application of a geometric relationship, *tangents of the angles of right triangles,* is often used to estimate distances to "inaccessible points." An often suggested procedure is:

1. Select an object "A" across the river to which you want to know the distance from where you stand at "B."

2. Walk along the shore at a right angle to a line between "A" and "B."

3. Continue until you reach a position ("C") at which "A" is 45 degrees (or 60 degrees or whatever degree you select) from your line of travel "BC."

4. Measure the distance between "C" and beginning point "B." Multiply by the appropriate tangent for the angle (tangent of 45 degrees is "1").

Difficulty can be encountered, however, in marking out a right angle and knowing if the angle at "C" is 60 degrees, 45 degrees, or whatever you select. A sighting board (merely a piece of plywood with 3 finish nails forming a 30- or 60-degree right triangle (or a 45-degree isosceles right triangle) can help, and the distances can be measured to a relatively high degree of accuracy.

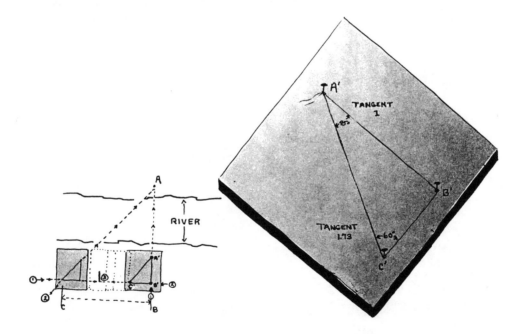

To obtain the right angle at "B":

Place the board at the beginning position ("B"). Student 1 should sight from B' through A' on the object ("A") across the river to *orient* the board. Student 2 should sight from B' through C' on the board and guide Student 3 to place a stake ("C") on a line forming a right angle.

To obtain the needed 60-degree (or 45-degree) angle, move the board along line "CB." When the apparent necessary distance is reached, Student 1 sights back from C' through B' to "B" to orient the board. Student 2 sights from C' through A' toward point "A." Move the board along the line "CB" until Student 2 can see "A" in the sights. The board is then in the correct position for point "C." The distance across the river to "A" is obtained by multiplying the distance "C" to "B" by the appropriate tangent (tangent of 60 degrees = 1.73; tangent of 45 degrees = 1).

Measuring the Tangents of Angles

The tangent of an angle (the side of a right triangle opposite an angle divided by the adjacent side) can be used to estimate tree or building heights, distances to "inaccessible points," etc.

Obviously, the tangent increases as the acute angle increases (see following illustration). In most cases, tangents of 30-, 45-, and 60-degree angles are used when estimating such distances and heights with children.

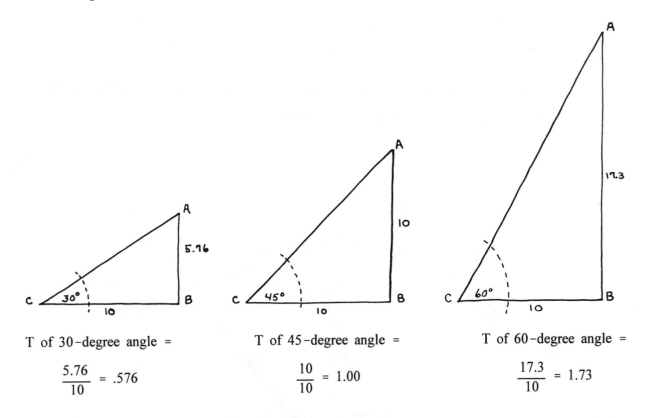

T of 30-degree angle =

$$\frac{5.76}{10} = .576$$

T of 45-degree angle =

$$\frac{10}{10} = 1.00$$

T of 60-degree angle =

$$\frac{17.3}{10} = 1.73$$

Students may wish to measure these and the tangents of other angles themselves. They can use a magnetic compass, transit, or a sighting device (see illustration on next page) to lay out right triangles with various sizes of acute angles.

1. Mark out a right angle ABC in the field. Stretch twine between points A and B and extend it an appropriate distance, perhaps, 100 meters (about 300 feet). Stretch twine between B and C, locating C exactly 10 meters (33 feet) from B.

2. To find the tangent for a 30-degree angle: Measure a 30-degree angle from C, with CB being one side and the other extending to inter- sect AB (at point D). The distance BD divided by distance CB (10 meters/33 feet) is the tangent of a 30-degree angle.

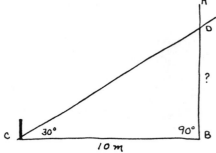

121

3. Student's tangent: _____ Textbook tangent:_____

    Reason for difference:_____

4. Repeat Step 2 using a 45-degree angle at C.

    Student's tangent _____ Textbook tangent _____

5. What is the tangent of a 60-degree angle?

    Student's tangent _____ Textbook tangent _____

6. If time permits, measure the tangent of angles of 10 degrees, 20 degrees, 30 degrees, 40 degrees, etc., on through to 80 degrees. Is there a pattern? If so, what is it?_____

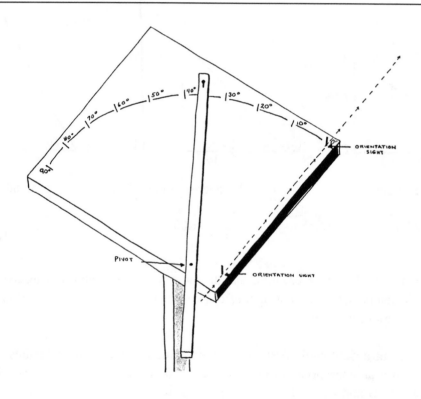

Geometric Principles in Map Construction

Introduction: Mapping the school or camp grounds clarifies concepts of maps and what they represent. It also provides an application for geometric principles.

Objectives: To construct a "scale map."
To experience the use of "non-standard" measuring devices.
To clarify "scale."
To apply the principle, *"if the three sides of a triangle are of fixed lengths, the shape of the triangle cannot be altered."*

Materials: Mapping paper (on a clipboard).
An inscribing compass and protractor for each person.
Several magnetic compasses.
Area to be mapped. (In an early attempt this might consist of an area about 15 meters (50 feet) square which contains a few trees or other items).

Procedure: 1. Place a line across the base of the paper, and divide it into equal segments of about 5 millimeters (0.2 inch). This is your "scale line."

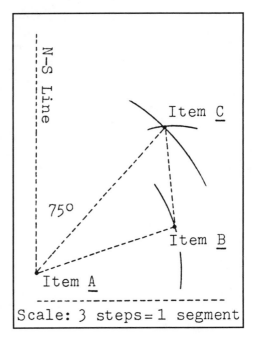

2. Select the size of map you wish to make. Step off the width and length of the area to be mapped. Arrive at a "scale" (expressed in steps per segment of the scale line).

Example: 1 scale line segment may represent 3 steps.

3. Position (on your map) one corner of your area (Item **A**). Lightly draw a north-south line through this point parallel to the edge of the paper.

4. The next item to be mapped (**B**) is related to **A** in distance and direction. To map the distance, count the steps between **A** and **B**, and spread the inscribing compass the appropriate interval on the scale line. Draw an arc on your map, using this as a radius and **A** as a center. **B** is located someplace on this arc.

5. Obtain the azimuth from **A** to **B**. Use a protractor to locate the position of **B** on the arc on your map. Once two items **A** and **B** have been mapped, no additional directional measurements are needed. Why?

6. To locate another item (**C**), step the distance between **A** and **C**, spread the compass the appropriate interval on the scale line, and draw an arc with **A** as the center. Repeat for the distance between **B** and **C**. **C** is at the intersection of the arcs.

NOTE: In the sketch, **B** is 24 steps from **A** and at an azimuth of 75 degrees. **C** is 38 steps from **A** and 18 steps from **B**.

The position of additional items or points can be mapped by utilizing any two previously mapped items as reference points.

Simple Machines: Outdoors

Objectives: To provide direct experiences with simple machines (levers, block and tackle, inclined planes, etc.).
To develop appreciation for these devices.
To use simple machines to do work.

Materials: Poles, planks, rope, pulleys, blocks, posts, objects to be moved, etc.

Preparation: Discuss hypothetical situations. Develop hypotheses for solving problems like these (sketch possible solutions):

1. To remove a person from under a fallen tree.

2. To move the butt of a fallen tree that blocks a road.

3. To move a heavy object (such as a car) several meters (feet).

4. To move a heavy object (that will not roll) a long distance.

5. To lift an object heavier than you are higher than your head.

6. To raise a heavy bucket (or person) from a well.

Activities: Arrange situations like the following to use, and test the children's solutions:

1. *Example:* A heavy fallen log or tree must be raised. (Students will suggest using a pole or pry bar.) Allow them to experiment to find a way to raise the tree, then raise it. (Analyze their experiments. Which were successful?)

   Discuss the relationship between the tree (the load), the block (the fulcrum), and the effort (the force). Sketch these relationships!

2. *Example:* Move the butt of a fallen tree away from its stump or off the trail. Approach and analyze this problem in the same manner as in No. 1.

3. *Example:* Move a heavy object such as a car (with brakes set). Consider levers, pulling with a rope, using a block and tackle, etc. Allow students to experiment to find a solution. One possible solution is to use the mechanical advantage of the "block and tackle."

4. *Example:* Move a heavy object (that can't be rolled) a long distance. What are the possibilities? How did the Egyptians move the stones they used in the pyramids? (A research question?) Would this approach work? Try it! How do we get the object onto the rollers? Does teamwork help?

Analysis: Other activities or situations can be arranged outdoors on playgrounds to challenge youngsters. Although solving these may be of educational value in the affective domain, little cognitive learning will occur until students and teachers make careful analyses of the mechanical principles being used.

Younger children may have to do little more than handle the apparatus to realize that they can do things with these machines that they cannot do without them. Intermediate-grade children may understand the relationships between machines used and "input" and "output." Upper-grade children should actually attempt to measure the forces and work being done and compute mechanical advantages.

Use Full-sized Models to Clarify Size Concepts

Do all children *really* understand when discussions deal with ideas such as the height of the Statue of Liberty, the size of the *Mayflower,* or the area of an acre? Just how large is a DC–10? Perhaps many of your students lack direct experience with the objects (or their sizes) about which they read, write, and speak.

To expect a child to memorize the fact that oak trees may grow 100 feet tall and to respond properly on the IBM® answer sheet is pointless if the child has no height concepts—and especially so, if the teacher also has none.

Teachers report that marking or staking out full-sized models on the schoolsite or campsite helps to give meaning to some of these elusive size and quantity concepts. These teachers often have their children measure out these objects and mark out their outline and other dimensions on the field with colored flags. Occasionally they will paint the outlines on a blacktop play area.

One trick used to accomplish the job quickly and effectively (and to involve all the children in a class) is to make each one responsible for marking out a different part or dimension of the model.

Before going to the field, the students have used an outline map of the object and have determined the distance they must mark. They know the object's relationship to a base line or starting point and to the sections being marked out by other members of the group.

Some possibilities: The *Mayflower* (or *Queen Elizabeth).*
The *Spirit of St. Louis.*
A DC–10.
The Statue of Liberty.
An acre of land.
A brontosaurus.
A whale.
A fallen sequoia tree.
The log cabin in which Abe Lincoln was born.

One model may be superimposed over another by using different colors of flags *(Mayflower* and DC–10) so as to provide size comparisons. Positioning the same number of children in the model as there were people aboard the *Mayflower,* for instance, is revealing.

XI. Nature Arts and Crafts

A number of books have been written about the use of natural materials in arts and crafts programs. These books and guides have served classroom teachers and camp leaders well over the decades. The availability of these resources, coupled with children's desires to create something of beauty/utility to take home, has resulted in arts and crafts being among the most popular activities of outdoor education and camping programs.

Included here are a few tips and suggestions that have been useful in providing experiences of this type. They include ideas for simple projects and discuss the ways that nature arts and crafts activities can be utilized to improve children's perceptions, understandings, and appreciations of the outdoors and the natural environment.

The activities suggested herein do not require the use of expensive tools or exotic materials. Indeed, both tools and materials for most of the projects are probably already in the environment of prospective users.

Nature Crafts in Outdoor Education

Objective: To use nature crafts to communicate skills, concepts, and knowledge.

Planning: Set the stage for creative crafts when planning the outdoor experience. As goals are being developed, pose questions such as "How can we use crafts projects to show others what we studied?" and "Where might we find materials to use for our crafts projects?" Such questions may assist students to observe more carefully and to collect more appropriate materials to use in these projects.

Help children with their "outdoor etiquette" and the conservation of natural resources. Some examples of such etiquette are:

1.   Be conservation conscious when collecting.

2.   Observe the law in collecting. It is unlawful in most parks to collect living things. Under certain conditions you may use dead things found on the ground.

3.   Carefully preserve the materials that you collect.

4.   Obtain permission before collecting on private property.

5.   Collect only materials that are in abundance.

6.   Observe the laws that protect many birds, flowers, plants, and animals. Become familiar with such laws.

7.   Do not collect in areas that are heavily used by people (such as near trails and buildings).

8.   Do not mar landscapes—don't chip on rock faces.

Learning such guidelines may help children to realize the importance of natural resources and be more concerned about pollution, destruction of property, and other abuses.

Projects in Social Studies

Have children make cosmetics, jewelry, tools, ornaments, and other items using native materials. Nuts, stones, wood, parts of plants and animals, and other native materials can be fashioned into useful and ornamental items of various cultures. Natural dyes can be made from grasses, seeds, nuts, flowers, etc., to provide color for wool and cotton materials. Tapestries can be made from yarn colored by these dyes. Rocks can be fashioned into crude tools.

The use of the axe and saw, such activities as lashing, rope making, weaving on homemade looms, basketry, and leather work, and the study of shelter building and fire building can be related to studies of early settlers.

Projects in Science

Wood carving helps one to understand wood hardness, grain, color, and texture. Cross-sections of trees may be sanded to show growth patterns, tree rings, layers of bark, and wood. Leaves and flowers can be pressed between layers of waxed paper or contact paper. These can be placed in decorative arrangements or kept for study. Plaster casts of animal tracks or leaf prints become "take home" souvenirs.

Wood and bark affected by insect boring and chewing can be used in decorative arrangements. Terrariums help to show relationships between plant growth and water cycles and can depict several kinds of environments (desert life, mosses, lichens, etc.), or they can be arranged for artistic appeal. Seeds, nuts and other fruits, leaves, and bark can be used in making jewelry, decorative arrangements, and other art forms, or they can be arranged to aid in identification.

Projects in Mathematics

Many lines, shapes, and designs are to be found in nature. Various designs can be seen in flower petal arrangements, the circular pattern of a stem, cross-section of the hexagon of a honeycomb cell, etc. Reoccurring patterns may be found in the petals of flowers or leaves. The general triangular silhouette of a blue spruce may be duplicated in the silhouette of a milkweed pod, in leaves of a cottonwood tree, or in petals of a trillium. These patterns can be captured through techniques such as smoke prints, blue prints, block prints, sketches, arrangements, collages, etc.

Print Projects

Stamp Prints

Stamps can be carved from materials such as potatoes, carrots, apples, leaves, and wood. These are constructed on the principle of a stamp and ink pad.

After the stamp is carved, press it into a coloring material (ink, water color, oil color, etc.) which has been soaked into a pad (such as a stamp pad) or left in a liquid or near-liquid state. After the stamp is soaked, press it onto paper, wood, cardboard, or some other porous material.

Experiment with several kinds of stamps and coloring materials, and develop patterns for decorating pictures, personalizing stationery and camp notebooks, etc.

Smoke Prints

Smoke printing is one of the most delicate of all print forms. It is a simple process, but it must be done carefully. Rub a thin layer of oil (vegetable oil or something similar) on a piece of paper. Next, light a candle, and move the oiled side of the paper near the top of the flame until it is black with soot.

Press a leaf on the smoked surface, and rub it well. Then place the leaf onto a piece of clean paper, stationery, etc. Cover with another paper, and rub over the entire area. Lift the paper carefully.

A fixative may be sprayed on the print after it has dried. Color may be added to prints by lightly dusting them with tempera powder immediately after they are made. Excess powder should be blown off.

Tracing Prints

Tracing prints may be made from leaves and similar items. Place the leaf on a flat surface with the vein side up. Cover with a paper, and rub a pencil or crayon over the paper, pressing down on the leaf. Broad, sweeping strokes or short, swift strokes are most effective.

Blueprints

Blueprint paper (a drafting supply material) may be used to obtain silhouettes (or patterns if more than one item is to be printed) of various plant parts such as leaves from trees, grasses, ferns, etc. Place the object on cardboard, masonite, or some other suitable material, and cover it with a piece of glass. Place the blue, sensitive side of the paper up. Hold, glass side up,

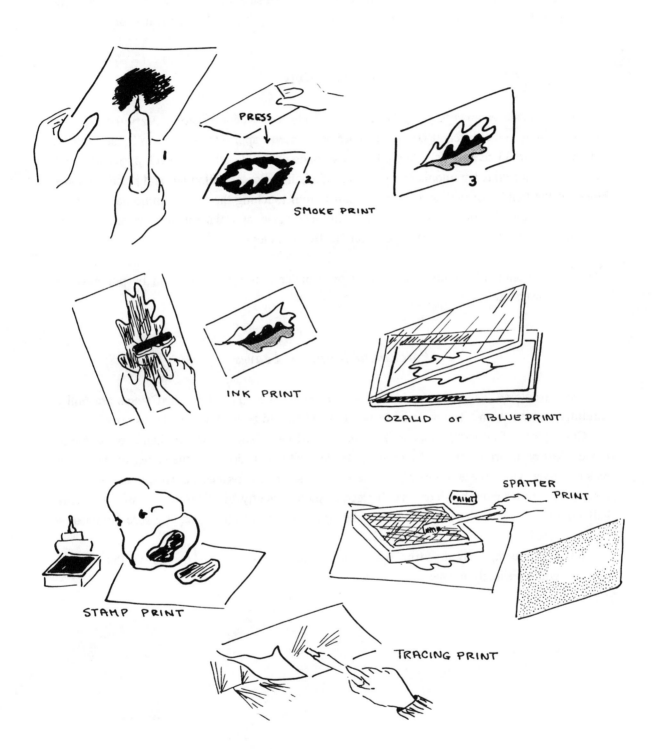

PRESS

SMOKE PRINT

INK PRINT

OZALID or BLUEPRINT

STAMP PRINT

SPATTER PRINT

PAINT

TRACING PRINT

and expose it to the sunlight from 30 seconds to 2 minutes, depending upon the intensity of the light. Then take it to a shady area, and immerse it, exposed side down, in a solution of water and one drop of hydrogen peroxide for about 30 seconds. Hang it on a line until it is dry.

Ozalid Prints

Repeat the above process, using Ozalid paper instead of blueprint paper. Vary the exposure time according to the different colors of paper being used: approximately 12 to 25 seconds for red paper, 20 to 35 seconds for blue, 40 to 50 seconds for black, etc. To develop, place a small amount of concentrated ammonia in the bottom of a half-gallon or gallon jar, and place a wooden block on the bottom of the jar to keep the paper from touching the liquid ammonia. With the print side in, loosely roll the paper into a cylindrical shape, and place it into the jar. Remove when the proper color and image appear (one to five minutes).

NOTE: An ammonia solution 28 percent or stronger is needed. This can be purchased in drugstores.

Parchment Mounted Leaves

Press a colored leaf or leaves in a book for about 24 hours. If the leaf stems are bulky, carefully remove them. The material to be mounted should be as thin and flat as possible.

Cut a piece of clear-type (not milky-type) waxed paper slightly larger than a facial tissue. Place a leaf or an arrangement of a group of leaves, with veins down, in the center of the waxed paper. Cover with a piece of one-ply, white facial tissue (some tissues are two-ply and some are three-ply). With a paint brush or a small piece of sponge, gently "dab" (do *not* brush) a half-and-half mixture of white glue and water over the entire surface of the tissue. Be sure the tissue is well saturated.

When it is completely dry, trim with a paper cutter or scissors. To improve the product, frame it with construction paper.

"Different" Print Projects

A Waxed Paper Leaf Sandwich is for showing not eating. Projects can be displayed in many ways, on the bulletin board, in notebooks, etc. They are most spectacular when taped to a window.

Materials: Waxed paper.   Small knife.
Leaves and/or small wild flowers.   Electric iron.
Various-colored crayons.   Heat-resistant pad.
Scissors.

Procedure: Cut a piece of waxed paper to the desired size, and lay it waxed side up on a heat-resistent pad. Place an arrangement of leaves and/or small wild flowers, etc., in the center of the paper.

Cut several very small pieces of various colored crayons, and place the pieces on the waxed paper surrounding the arrangement of leaves or flowers. Cover with another piece of waxed paper (waxed side down).

Apply a warm (not hot) iron to the paper. (Experimentation will reveal the proper setting.) Simply lift the iron to move it from place to place (do not glide iron as you do when you iron clothing). The ironing will effectively seal the two pieces of waxed paper and also will melt the small pieces of colored crayons, leaving a nice stained-glass effect.

A Spider Web Print is a very simple but effective arts and crafts project. Many different web patterns can be found that will provide exciting projects. The average spider can replace a web in a short time, so the loss of a web is not a big problem for the spider.

Materials: Can of spray paint *(not* quick-drying).
Colored construction paper.
Spider webs.

Procedure: Find a good spider web. Make sure the spider is gone and that there are no captured insects in it.

Holding the can of spray paint 30 to 45 centimeters (12 to 18 inches), depending upon the type of nozzle, away from the web, spray first the front and then the back of the web.

Immediately bring a piece of construction paper up to the web from the rear and clip the anchor strands. The painted web will stick to the paper, and the colored paint will show up effectively if the construction paper is of a good contrasting color.

Sketching in Nature

Real enjoyment is achieved when an individual feels the freedom to sketch without concern about the final product. Encourage children to make their own interpretations, leaving out what they do not like and emphasizing what is of interest to them. When you convey this attitude to the children, it helps them to realize that they do not need to make their pictures like any other picture.

Sketching
Equipment: Large sheets of paper (30 × 45 cm/12 × 18 in.)—newsprint or drawing paper or any clean surface.

Boards—heavy cardboard, masonite, or similar material.

Sketching materials—soft pencil (#2B is best), chalk, crayon, or charcoal from the campfire.

Soft eraser.

Fixative—especially if using chalk or charcoal.

Suggestions
for
Sketching: *Using a Pencil.* Position pencil across the hand, not between the fingers as for writing. Use the broad edge of the pencil rather than the fine point. A stone or a piece of sandpaper may be helpful to get a broad edge on the pencil.

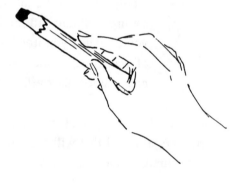

Selecting a Subject. Encourage the students to select something in nature that is of interest to them for their sketch. Remember that "beauty is in the eyes of the beholder." Using a finder or shaping the hands like a window will help them select a view. Emphasize that they should select a scene that has an item near the center (to keep the viewer's eyes from leaving the picture). Objects such as a fence, road, river, etc., in a foreground position and leading to the area of interest will help hold the viewer's attention.

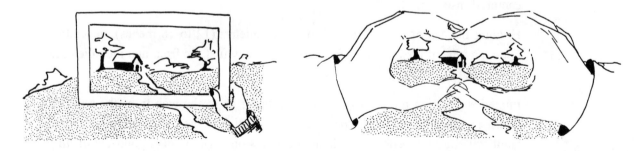

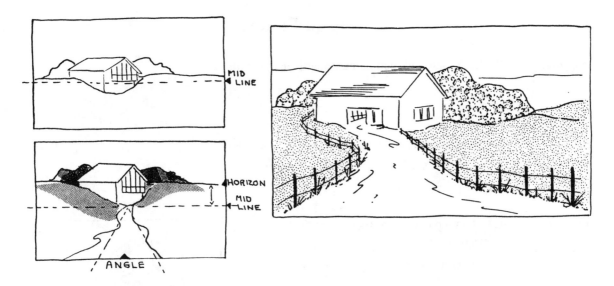

Making the Sketch. Now the students are ready to translate what they saw in the finder. Have them begin by blocking in the picture by simply sketching a few lines locating the various objects in the scene. (This should take no longer than two minutes.) Next, tell them to decide on light and dark areas. Remind them that emphasis such as more detail and stronger lines should be used in the area of interest to attract the viewer to this part of the picture.

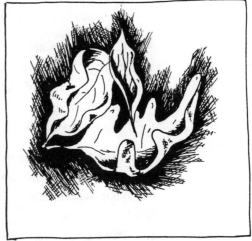

Suggest that they notice where the light (sun) comes from and to include the appropriate shadows—a suggestive line or two will often be sufficient and eliminate the need to detail each shadow.

Sketching should be fun! Make it an enjoyable experience for your students. Take into consideration their experience levels and skills. Avoid frustrating students and thereby hindering their self-expression.

A Nature Picture

Supplies: Backing material such as cardboard or masonite.

String.

Glue.

Poster paint.

Natural materials such as dried grasses, corn shucks and kernels, sand and pebbles, twigs, and seeds.

A knife.

Directions:

1. Cut a piece of cardboard (or the material being used for backing) to the desired picture size.

2. Paint the background a solid color or spatter paint it.

3. Place natural materials on the dry painted background to form a picture (or perhaps an interesting arrangement). When you have the desired design, glue the materials to the backing.

4. Cut dry branches or sticks several centimeters (inches) longer than each side of the backing. Lash them together to form the frame for your picture.

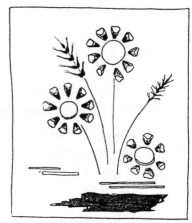

5. Lash, tack, or glue the backing to the back of the frame. Tie a string to two corners of the frame so that your picture may be hung on a wall.

Variations:

1. Paint clouds, sky, and lakes on the background, and then fill in the trees, buildings, paths, and rocks by gluing dried natural materials on this painted background.

2. A three-dimensional type of picture can be made in much the same way by using a cardboard box.

Working with Wood

Soft woods such as white pine, basswood, aspen, and sumac are good woods for beginners to use for carving. Apple, cherry, walnut, osage orange, red cedar, and hickory make beautiful carvings, but are hard and more difficult to work with.

Equipment: Sharp knives.
Coping saw.
Sandpaper.

NOTE: For more difficult carvings, wood chisels and other woodworking tools may be necessary.

Directions:

1. Decide upon an object to shape.

2. Choose a piece of wood about the correct size and shape to conserve materials and reduce the amount of work required.

3. Sketch the outline of the object on the wood.

4. Using a sharp knife, and cutting away from you as much as possible, rough carve around the outline. (A coping saw is often helpful in preliminary shaping.)

5. The "finish" carving should be carefully and slowly done to prevent the splitting and chipping of the wood.

6. Sand or leave carving marks as desired.

7. To finish, apply linseed oil or stain or leave untreated as desired.

Suggestions for Beginners:

Carve such objects as letter openers, animal shapes, pins, and tags.

Suggestions for Advanced Carvers:

Carve such objects as complete animals, beach clogs, and totem poles.

XII. Plants

A focus of plant studies should be on the realization that plants are the basis of all food supplies. Another is to develop appreciation for the diversity of plant forms.

At another level, one should concentrate on helping youths to do the work of the scientist—observing, classifying, comparing, explaining, etc. These are general skills; whereas, plants are the most serviceable material to be used in specific scientific practices.

This series contains samples of ways plants may be studied outdoors with children. Teachers should develop and use their own variations of these simple formats. The *fact sheets* are designed to arouse curiosities and to serve as the basis for examination, data gathering, and discussion.

The *clue-chart* approach is very useful. And later, the clues students list can be used with keys to identify the plants in question. Sometimes, only a single trait (such as the leaf of a tree) needs to be examined to arrive at a correct identification, with other characteristics serving only as additional descriptors. However, some characteristics must be followed throughout the growing season to be useful in identification.

A Fact List for a Tree

1. Observe a tree any time during the year:

   a. Name of tree: _____

   b. Height: _____ meters _____ feet

   c. Diameter of trunk at one-meter height: _____ cm

   d. Twigs opposite or alternate: _____

   e. Estimated age of tree: _____ years

2. Observe a tree when it is leafed out:

   a. Leaves opposite or alternate: _____

   b. Leaves simple or compound: _____

   c. Leaf edges smooth, toothed, or lobed: _____

   d. Leaves smooth or rough: _____

   e. Make a print or rubbing of a leaf.

3. Observe a tree throughout the growing season:

   a. Date of appearance of new leaves: _____

   b. Date of appearance of flowers: _____

   c. Date seeds became recognizable: _____

   d. Date when ripe fruits fell to the ground: _____

   e. Autumn colors of leaves: _____

   f. Date leaves fell: _____ to _____

LEAF — SIMPLE

LEAFLETS — COMPOUND

MARGIN — SMOOTH / TOOTHED

BRANCHING — OPPOSITE / ALTERNATE

A Fact List for a Stump

Before it decomposes, a stump can offer clues about its past. Every year a tree adds a growth ring to its diameter. When the tree is cut down, the rings are seen as concentric circles on the stump. Rings vary in size depending on many environmental factors, including weather, injuries, competition, etc. Studying a stump can be an interesting way to combine history and biology.

1. Approximately how long ago was the tree felled? _____

    In what year was that? _____

2. Why was it cut down? _____

3. Which way did it fall? _____

4. How old was the tree when it fell? _____

5. Was the tree's growth the same each year? _____

6. If not, in which years did the tree make good growth? _____

    In which years did it make poor growth? _____

7. Are there signs of injury to the tree when alive? _____

    If so, what are they? _____

    When did the injuries occur? _____

8. Locate important years on the stump by counting back years of growth in the rings.

    _____

9. Find and list signs of decay. _____

    _____

10. Take a rubbing of the stump *to take back with you.*

11. Find out about the weather and the history of those years when unusual events seemed to happen to the tree (a forest fire, logging, unusual amounts of rainfall, etc.).

A Clue Chart for Trees and Shrubs

	Specimen	Leaves	Bark	Branching	Flowers	Fruit	Buds	Other
1.								
2.								
3.								

In the appropriate space above, provide a description (using words or sketches as you wish) of the leaves, bark, branching, etc., of each of the trees or shrubs you examine. Some clues to look for are described below.

Leaves: needles/leaves
alternate/opposite
simple/compound
length in centimeters
(inches)
number of leaflets
edges, smooth/lobed/
toothed
top and bottom,
smooth/hairy

Bark: color
plates/ridges/projections

Branching: alternate/opposite

Flowers: catkins—drooping/erect
size, shape
number of petals
form of petals
colors, odors, taste

Fruit: size, kind, color, shape
type of cover or husk

Buds: opposite/alternate
size, color, shape
texture (fuzzy/waxy)
scales

Other: height, shape outline
hardwood/softwood

If all clues are to be noted, data must be collected throughout an entire year. However, some clues such as the leaves may provide enough information to enable one to determine what species is being studied.

A Clue Chart for Herbaceous (Not-woody) Flowers

	Specimen	Leaves	Sepals	Petals	Stamens	Pistils	Inflorescence
1.							
2.							
3.							

Flowers are the most conspicuous part of herbaceous plants. Often a plant may be identified by its flower alone. A good hand lens is helpful in the detailed task of identifying flower parts. Sometimes, individual flowers are very tiny; and, in such composites as dandelions and daisies, they grow very close together and appear as a single flower. For each specimen, provide a description of the clue in the proper space in the clue chart. This clue chart may also be used for partial identification of woody plants.

Leaves: shape, size
number on stem
arrangement on stem
shape of stem

Sepals: green/petal-colored
number, color, length, shape
united/separated

Petals: number, color, size, shape
united/separated
alike/different

Stamens: (male part)
number, color, shape
attached/unattached to petals

Pistils: (female part)
number, color, size, shape
segments to style
compartments
attachment above/below petals

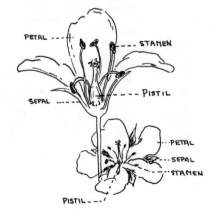

Inflorescence: one/more flowers on a head
arrangement of flowers on a stem
arrangement of stems and leaves
all flowers alike/different

A Clue Chart for Twigs in Winter

	Specimen	Twigs	Buds	Leaf Scars	Other
1.					
2.					
3.					

In the appropriate space above, provide a description of each specimen you examine (using words or sketches as you wish) of the twigs and buds in their winter condition. Although examining twigs requires an eye for detail, it is not too difficult to do. Some clues to look for are described below.

Twigs: color of last year's growth
color of previous year's growth
opposite/alternate
shape, thickness
texture, markings

Buds: opposite/alternate
color, size, shape
number of scale leaves
sticky/hairy/smooth
terminal bud/no terminal bud

Leaf Scars: size, shape
pattern
if opposite—meeting/not
meeting

Other: presence of thorns/catkins
last year's fruit
peculiarities of bark—shaggy/
ridged/protrusions

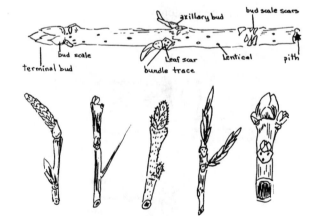

A Clue Chart for Fruits and Seeds

	1	2	3
Mechanisms for Dispersal			
Size			
Color			
Shape			
Kind of Fruit			
Texture			
Placement of Seeds			
Individual Seeds			

Seeds are an important part of plants. Not only do they have the ability to start new plants, but they also serve as food for people, animals, and birds. Sometimes (especially in winter), plants can be identified by their seeds. Some seeds occur singly, while others grow in clusters. In the appropriate space above, provide a description (using clues) for each specimen you examine. Some clues to look for are described below.

Mechanisms for Dispersal: tufts of hair/hooks/burs/ thin membranous wings

Size: in centimeters/in inches

Color: red/yellow/brown dull/bright

Shape: square/round/oval/ heart-shaped

Kind of Fruit: fleshy (berry)/woody (nut)/papery

Texture: rough/smooth/hard/soft/fuzzy/ waxy/papery

Placement of Seeds: inside/outside fruit inside shell

Individual Seeds: size, shape number in/on fruit number of parts (one/two)

A Plant Observation Project

Do your students realize how much things change and develop from day to day? Do they look, but not see? Do they need more experiences that require them to closely observe, examine, and describe what they see? If so, try an observational project with a plant as the focus.

Have each student select a plant or a part of a plant, such as a bud, to examine and observe for a five-minute period each day. Have them write reports explaining everything that happens to the plant, measuring and recording any growth that occurs. Continue this activity for several weeks.

The projects may be undertaken at the school, at a campsite, or in the home. Advise the students to select items that might show appreciable change and to not "bite off" too much. Before beginning the project, refresh the students' memories about the use of scientific controls and the design of data-gathering and record-keeping systems.

Most success results when items like the following are selected:

1. A rosebud as it expands, blossoms, and withers.
2. A hickory bud as it unfolds in the spring.
3. A corn, pumpkin, or other rapidly growing plant or vine.
4. Events that take place on a window or a particular square of the lawn.
5. A plant community on a rotting log or stump.

Expect some difficulty for several days until the students begin to see and perceive. As they become more familiar with their projects, they will have more to report. Then, each day, some of them will have exciting news or discoveries to relate to the rest of the groups such as "My pumpkin plant grew 7 centimeters (3 inches) yesterday." "My bud is opening." "I didn't know there were so many ants!"

Eventually, the students will become interested in projects other than their own and will want to be kept informed about them. Some will want explanations for what they observe. Questions will arise that can be answered only by returning for additional observations or by consulting references. The ultimate goal is to be able to accurately report to others the events and changes that occur.

XIII. Outdoor Recreation

Important components of outdoor education and camping programs, whether they be school, summer or private, are recreational activities. These may have many educational outcomes.

No attempt is made here to cover all of outdoor recreation. The tips and suggestions included here, however, should assist leaders wishing to include singing, nature games, and square dancing in their programs.

Singing in the Outdoors

The joy and happiness of an outdoor education experience is often expressed through song. Many children love to sing about the good times at camp or outdoor education center.

Their songs take forms that range from the patriotic *"This Land Is Your Land"* to the simplest action song *"Do Your Ears Hang Low?"* The type and kind of song used will vary with the group or song leader. The following suggestions may be helpful for beginners.

1. *Seating arrangement.* Arrange the seats in a semicircle to give you the best eye contact with every singer. It also makes a group division possible for rounds or parts.

2. *Analysis of the song.* Briefly analyze the song for the singers. Does it tell a story? What is its background? Does it apply to the world of today or yesterday? Does it merely suggest a mood? Does it relate to the outdoors?

3. *Type of song.* Select some songs that are indigenous to where your group lives or to the local area. Select both familiar songs and new ones.

4. *Pitch of songs.* Choose a pitch for each song that will place the melody within the range of the majority of the singers.

5. *The beat.* Establish the "beat" and be responsible for maintaining it. The students can help maintain it by tapping their feet or clapping their hands.

6. *Leading a familiar song:*

    a. Announce the song.

    b. Make pertinent remarks about it and the way it should be sung.

    c. Give the pitch and begin.

    Once started, don't stop unless the situation is hopeless. Minor flaws are not reason enough to interrupt, but use discretion as to the number of times to sing the song or how many stanzas to use.

7. *Presenting an unfamiliar song:*

    a. Teach short and simple songs by rote. Be sure to have access to written words for longer songs.

    b. Teach a song that can be grasped in a few hearings.

    c. Sing the song through once.

150

d. Ask the group to sing along the second time.

e. Have all repeat the words in rhythm.

f. Break the song into phrases, and sing each phrase.

g. Sing the entire song.

8. *Social etiquette on the part of the leader:*

a. Avoid rigidity.

b. Be enthusiastic and forget yourself.

c. Be patient under trying circumstances.

d. Check up on mistakes as you go along. Enjoy a laugh over an obvious error.

e. Discipline the group by cajolery into a high standard of performance. Give a word of praise whenever possible.

f. Establish a congenial atmosphere. Avoid mannerisms that distract.

g. Aim at singing with spirit, but do not permit it to deteriorate into raucousness.

h. Keep just a little ahead of the group.

i. Be respectful for the art, and refuse to identify with what is musically in poor taste.

Obviously, the song leader has much responsibility for ensuring the singers a good time as well as an experience of enduring satisfaction. If the leader expects the best from the members of the group, they will usually respond.

Some Songs for School and Camp

The titles of some of the longtime camp songs that are favorites of children and leaders are listed below and are to be found in various song books. The beginning song leader should acquire several of these books initially and continually add to the collection. The figure in parentheses after the titles in the "Rounds – Canons" group refers to the number of parts in the song.

Rounds – Canons

Early to Bed (3)
Fare Thee Well (4)
Frog Round (4)
Good Night to You All (3)
Grasshoppers Three (3)
Happy Days (4)
Hello (4)
Hello-Hello-Hello (4)
Hey, Ho! Nobody Home (3)
Ho Every Sleeper Waken (3)
Hungarian Round (3)
Hunting Song (4)
I Love the Mountains (3)
Johney! Johney! (2)
Let Us Sing Together (4)
Lovely Evening (3)
Make New Friends (4)
Merrily, Merrily (4)
Morning Is Come (4)
Music Alone Shall Live (2)
Now All the Woods Are Waking (4)
Oh, How Lovely Is the Evening (3)
Puffer Billies (4)
Rise Up O' Flame (8)
Sing Together (3)
The Little Bells (4)
To Open Their Trunks (3)
Whip-poor-will (3)
White Sands and Grey Sands (3)
Who Comes Laughing? (3)

Action and Fun Songs

Canoe Song
Cuckoo
Downright, Upright
Down the River
Hole in the Bucket
In a Cabin in a Woods
Little Bells of Westminster
One Finger, One Thumb
Over the Meadows
Sarasponda
Six Little Ducks
The Climate
The Hunter
The Instrument Song
My Hat It Has Three Corners

Campfire Songs

Campfire Closing
Each Camp Fire Lights Anew
Peace of the River
Rise Up O' Flame
Sing Your Way Home
Tell Me Why
Who Loves the Rain?
Witchcraft

Vesper and Sacred Songs

All Thru the Night
Bed Is Too Small
Children's Prayer
Day Is Dying
Dona Nobis Pacem
Evening Star
Green Grow the Rushes
Joyful, Joyful
Kum Ba Ya
Now Comes the Hour
Now the Day Is Over
Ranger Song
Slumber, Slumber
Tallis Canon
Taps
Vesper Hymn
Were You There?
Whip-poor-will

Graces

God Created a New Day
Gratitude Grace (Doxology Tune)
Morning Is Come (Noon, Evening)
Thank You for the World So Sweet
Wayfarer's Grace
Wesley Grace (Doxology Tune)

American Folksongs

A-Jogging Along
A-Roving
Canoe Song
Erie Canal
Little Wheel
Ol' Texas
Navajo's Happy Song
Riddle Song

Spirituals

All Night All Day
He's Got the Whole World
Jacob's Ladder
My Lord, What a Morning
Nobody Knows the Trouble I've Seen
Oh, Won't You Sit Down?
Standing in the Need of Prayer
Swing Low, Sweet Chariot
Two Wings
Wayfaring Stranger

Patriotic Songs

America
America the Beautiful
Four Strong Winds
This Land Is Your Land

Art Songs

No Man Is an Island
Now Comes the Hour
Poor and Carefree Stranger
Riddle Song

Hiking Songs

Caravan Song
Marching to Pretoria
Swinging Along
The Happy Wanderer
Upward Trail

Nature Games

Nature games are fun as well as educational and can be an effective device to create good relationships between individuals and to develop group cohesiveness. Games should be an integral part of the outdoor education program. Their potential contribution to a program lies in these areas:

1. To reinforce learning from previous sessions.

2. To develop skills and appreciations.

3. To provide entertainment during free time and recreation periods.

4. To provide variety to one's teaching.

5. To stimulate new interests.

Nature games can be effective in many settings and often provide a welcome change of pace for all age groups. They are a valid activity in themselves and should not be used as a substitute for nature study.

Solving problems through observation is a unique experience in itself and can be fun when it takes the form of a game. The following are important when organizing and leading nature activities that center around a game:

1. Consider the desires of the group participating in the activity.

2. Strive for maximum participation from the group.

3. Divide large groups into small teams to ensure more participation.

4. Properly supervise all activities.

5. Place the emphasis on *observations* (rather than on definite, previously learned responses).

The following games may provide ideas for leaders.

Hunting Games

Curio Collector. Call the name of something to be found (a stump of a tree more than 100 years old or a hollow log). The players scatter to find the object. The first to find it calls out. Lead a group examination and discussion of the object. Then name the next object to be found, and repeat the procedure.

Bug Bomb. Divide students into teams of three or four individuals. Each team is to have a container for its "bug collection." The teams then attempt to fill this "bug bomb" with as many different types of "bugs" that can be found. Specify a time limit, and develop a point system for each type of bug. Permit only one bug of a type to be counted.

Nature Near and Far. List 20 or 30 items to be found along a trail and assign a score to each item: (bird nest, 10 points; butterfly, 5 points; animal track, 5 points; etc.). The *first* player to observe and report one of these items receives the score for that item.

Scavenger Hunt. Divide children into pairs. Give each pair a list of nature items to find. The first team back with a correct and complete list wins. Include certain kinds of leaves, rocks, seeds, etc. Omit items you do not want to be picked. A variation is to have each team bring in items with names beginning with every letter of the alphabet.

Leaf Scavenger Hunt. List the names of 10 or more common trees at the campsite. The first player or team to bring in a leaf from each kind of tree is declared the winner. Give the younger children a leaf, and ask them to locate a tree that has a similar leaf.

Numbers in Nature

Secret Numbers. Place notes along a designated route, each note containing directions for securing a certain number or numeral considered to be the "secret number," known only to you. If all observations are made and all directions followed correctly, the sum of the numbers secured should equal the secret number. (Example: This tree is a sugar maple. If its leaves are arranged in twos opposite each other on the twig, the secret number is 10. If they are alternate [not opposite], the secret number is 5. The next note will be found under the skin of a large stump. Continue along the trail.)

Location of Species

Unnatural Nature. "Doctor up" a number of plants (tie oak leaves on a hickory tree, pine cones on a spruce, black-eyed susans on a thistle, etc.). Give the teams a limited (specify) time to identify as many of these as possible.

Stake a Claim. Introduce this activity after a discussion of the characteristics of a class or group of plants. (Example: Grasses tend to have round stems which are enclosed in the leaf; wind-pollinated nodes; and flowers with no color, nectar, or odor.) Stake off small areas. Divide the children into teams, and assign an area to each team. Instruct each team to find as many different species or types as it can in its own area within a specified time. Point systems can be used. Knowledgeable students may write down the names of those they find as well as count them.

Games

Animal Games

Open field, nature, or animal games help to enhance study in many subject matter areas.

Animal Blindman's Bluff. Have the players form a circle. Blindfold one player. This person should stand in the center of the circle. Instruct the other players to circle around the blindfolded person until he or she claps twice, signalling them to stop. Have the blindfolded player point toward a member of the circle, and have that player make the sound of a specific animal as requested by the blindfolded player. Tell the blindfolded player to try to guess the identity of the person making the animal sound. If he or she doesn't identify the player correctly, continue the game with the same person blindfolded. If the blindfolded person does identify the player correctly, he or she changes places with the player in the circle. Blindfold that player, and continue playing with a new blindfolded player.

Animal Chase. Mark off two pens or "safe areas" some distance apart in a field. Assign names of common animals to the players so that several players will have the same name, and have them assemble at one of the "safe areas." Designate one player to be "it" or the "chaser." Instruct the "chaser" to call the name of an animal, and tell the players having that name to try to get to the other "safe area" without being tagged or caught by the "chaser." Have the "animal" being caught or tagged become the new "chaser," and have the old "chaser" join the other "animals."

Catch the Fish. Draw a line near one end of a field. Draw a second line parallel to the first about 20 meters (about 65 feet) away. Divide the players equally into two groups, and have them face each other across the open space between the lines. Appoint one group to be the "net" and the other group to be the "fish." Have the "net" form a long line by clasping hands, and have the "net" attempt to catch the "fish." Instruct the "fish" to move forward to swim upstream across the open spaces and through the "net" without getting trapped. Inform the "fish" that they cannot break the "net" by forcing the hands to be unclasped, but that they may attempt to go under or around while the "net" tries to encircle them. (If any of the "net" players unclasp their hands and break the "net," have all the players return to the starting line and begin again.) All "fish" that are caught are out of the game. Continue the play until all "fish" are caught—then reverse the roles, and continue the game.

Chickadee-dee. Fill a grain or potato sack with leaves, hay, or straw, and tie shut. Blindfold one player. Have this player take the bag and stand in the center of a circle made up of the remaining players. Instruct the players in the circle to quietly sneak up to the blindfolded player, one at a time, and whisper "Chickadee-dee" close to the person's ear. Tell the blindfolded player to swing the bag and attempt to strike the whispering player. Have the "hit" player exchange places with the blindfolded player.

156

Skin the Snake. Have the players stand in a line, one behind the other, a short distance apart. Instruct them to bend forward, stretch one hand backwards between their legs and, with their other hand, grasp the hand of the player in front of them (who has assumed the same position). When all are in position, have the line begin to back up. (The grasped hands are retained throughout the activity.) Instruct the player at the end of the line to lie on his or her back while the others walk backwards astride the player lying down until the next player can go no further. Then have this player lie down with the first player's head between his or her legs. Continue having them back up and lie in a straight line. Have the player that lay down last get up, walk astride the line toward the front, raising the next player to his or her feet, and so on, until all are standing in their original positions.

Hound and the Rabbit. Arrange players in groups of three with their hands on each other's shoulders to form a small circle to represent a "hollow tree." Place another player who is a "rabbit" within the "hollow tree." Be sure there is one more "rabbit" than "hollow trees." Designate another player to be the "hound." Instruct the "hound" to chase the "rabbit" who isn't in a "tree." Inform the "rabbit" being chased that he or she can run into a tree that is already occupied, thus causing that "rabbit" to be the one who is being chased and trying to find safety in another "hollow tree." Explain that if the "hound" tags a "rabbit" outside the "hollow tree," the tagged "rabbit" them becomes the "hound," and the "hound" becomes a "rabbit." Also, if the "hound" finds an empty "hollow tree," the "hound" can move into it and become a "rabbit," and the "rabbit" left out then becomes the "hound." Instruct all the "rabbits" to be constantly moving across the field looking for new trees for shelter and, in order to give each player a chance to play all parts, stop the game long enough for the "rabbits" to change places with the "hollow trees."

Bird, Beast, or Fish. Have the players sit on the ground in a circle, faces to the inside. Select one player to stand in the center with a ball made of crushed paper or a knotted up handkerchief. Instruct the center player to throw the ball at a seated player and quickly say, "Bird, beast, or fish," and then immediately specify one of the three; for example, "bird." Explain to the group that the player who is hit by the ball must name a bird and that, as the game progresses, the player hit by the ball must name a bird, beast, or fish that had not previously been named by another player. Failure to do this causes that player to change places with the center player and become "it." Other versions may include subjects such as trees, flowers, rocks, or clouds.

Moving Games

Chair Cover. Seat the players in a circle (on chairs, logs, or benches). Select one player to stand in the center, with the other players occupying all the seats. Instruct the player in the center to call out, "Change to the left" or "Change to the right." Tell the seated players to quickly rise and move one seat to the left, or to the right, as directed. Explain that the center player should rush to try to get a seat. If he or she succeeds, the player left without a seat must go to the center and become "it." This is especially good for younger students; it is helpful in teaching them "left" and "right" directions.

Human Hurdle. Divide the players into two teams, and assign a number to each player (1, 2, 3, etc.), duplicating the numbers for each team. Have the players lie on the ground to form a circle (face down, feet outward, and arms close to the body). Explain that when you give a signal, player No. 1 of both teams should rise and jump over every player in succession on their respective teams. When No. 1 returns to the original place in the circle, he or she should lie down again in position. As soon as a player is jumped over, that player should rise and jump over every player. The team that completes the sequence first is the winner.

Chinese Get Up. Have the players pair up and sit back to back locking arms. Instruct them to attempt to stand up erect, keeping their arms locked together. As a pair succeeds in standing up, add a third individual. Each time a group is successful, add another player. Continue adding players until the goal is no longer achieved by any of the groups.

IMPORTANT: Many of these games and activities require the students to move about, sometimes swiftly. Teachers should always be alert to the potential hazards and student behaviors that can lead to injury. Care should be taken to assure that students are constantly supervised and that sites chosen for activities of this type are safe and free of obstacles and objects on which the students could fall or be injured.

Folk Dancing for Fun

Dancing is a leisure-time activity in every country in the world. In some places it may involve strange body movements in rhythm to weird music. In some countries the movements are slow and deliberate, while in others the movement is rapid and complex. But whatever it is like and wherever it may occur, people participate in dance because of the enjoyment they receive from it.

In early America, folk dancing took several different forms such as couple dances, square dances, circle dances, and contras. In recent years there has been a revival of interest in folk dancing, and today there are many groups throughout the United States which meet regularly for this purpose.

There is much to be derived from folk dancing. Probably the most important is the enjoyment that people receive while they participate. It does help to build group spirit, as everyone usually takes part, and it gives all participants the possibility to enjoy themselves. Participation is not limited to only the popular and the good looking. There also is much that can be learned about the countries in which the dances originated because the dances usually tell something about the cultures and way in which the people live.

American square dances are usually composed of three parts: the introduction, the figure, and the chorus. The caller directs the action either with a singing call or with a patter call, and is responsible, as a leader, to organize the program, help people gain the necessary skills, and foster an atmosphere in which participants can enjoy themselves.

The various forms of folk dancing are often associated with outdoor education resident experiences. The following pages deal with:

1. Suggestions for folk dance leaders.

2. Basic folk dance steps and formations.

3. Suggested dances.

Suggestions for Folk Dance Leaders

1. Hold the dance in a room of adequate size which can be properly ventilated.

2. Have good equipment (a variable speed record player and a microphone for large groups).

3. Arrange the sequence of dances to give you a variety which does not drag or become too strenuous.

4. Start with simple dances with new groups and familiar dances with advanced groups. Remember that people enjoy doing things in which they have developed some competency.

5. Keep breaks and trimmings to a minimum until you know your group.

6. Use mixers and ice-breakers to begin the evening.

7. Be patient—square dancing may be difficult for some of the group.

8. Get the attention of the group before you give directions.

9. Use demonstration teams or groups where possible, but do not make the demonstration a show of complicated steps and frills.

10. Have the dancers walk through a dance to help them learn new dances.

11. Slow down the music while the group is learning, and speed it up as it develops skill.

12. Speak clearly, and give complete, precise instructions.

13. Be prepared to anticipate trouble spots and to handle them.

14. Stop the dance and explain the step rather than continue when the group is confused.

15. Do not tell jokes or make comments that embarrass any of the dancers.

Basic Folk Dance Steps and Formations

The Square: The square consists of four couples standing on the four sides of a square, facing the center. The lady is on the gentleman's right, and each couple should be about 3 meters (9 feet) from the opposite couple. The couple with its back to the music is known as the "head" couple or the "number one" couple.

The Contra: The contra consists of two lines of dancers facing each other. One line is composed of gentlemen and the other of ladies. This formation is used in dances like the Virginia reel.

Square Dance Figures

1. *Circle Left*—All join hands and circle left.

2. *Promenade*—Using skating position, partners cross arms in front and join hands, right hand to right hand and left hand to left hand.

3. *Simple Do-si-do*—A gentleman and a lady (with arms folded in front of them) approach each other, pass back-to-back to the right, and back up to their original places.

4. *Grand Right and Left*

    a. The lady is to the gentleman's right.
    b. Face your partner, and extend your right hand.
    c. Walk forward, and passing to the right, extend your left hand to the person coming toward you.
    d. Give your left hand to this person, and pass to the right. Extend your right hand to the next person, and continue till you meet your partner.

5. *Allemande Left*

    a. Same formation as above.
    b. Lady to the left is known as the corner.
    c. The gentlemen face left, and the ladies face right (back-to-back).
    d. Extend your left hand, take your corner's left hand, and walk once around and back to where you started.

6. *Right and Left Through*

    a. Same formation as above.
    b. Extend your right hand to the person opposite you, and walk past, extending your left hand to your partner. Turn around to face the direction from whence you came, and repeat back to place.

7. *Ladies' Chain*

    a.   Two couples face each other with the ladies on the right.

    b.   The ladies join right hands and pass each other on the right.

    c.   Each gentleman extends his left hand to the lady and takes her left hand, reaches out with his right arm, places it around her waist, and leads her forward and around till they both face back from whence they came, and repeats to place.

8. *The Swing*

    a.   Join hands or link elbows with your partner, and walk around clockwise.

    b.   *Buzz Step Dance Position*

        (1)   Face your partner, and place the outside of your right feet together.

        (2)   Now take hands in ballroom dance position.

        (3)   Put weight on the right foot with the left toe in back of the right heel, and shove yourself around clockwise. Lean slightly back and slightly away from the waist up.

            (a)   Option. Ladies, place your right hand on your partner's left shoulder, and Gents, place yours upon her hip.

            (b)   Link right elbows, and swing with buzz step.

9. *Balance*

    a.   Option 1.

        (1)   Face your partner.

        (2)   Give your right hand to your partner.

        (3)   Step forward on your right foot, bringing your left foot up to it, and with a slight bounce, step back on the left foot, and bring the right foot back to it, and bounce.

    b.   Option 2.

        (1)   Face your partner.

        (2)   Step on your right foot, and brush your left foot across in front of your right foot.

        (3)   Step on your left foot, and brush your right foot across in front of your left foot.

        (4)   Do this to a bounce.

    c.   Option 3.

        (1)   Hold your partner's right hand.

        (2)   Nod your head. (Honor your Partner.)

Folk Dances

Couple Dances

1. *Jesse Polka* (Calico Polka)

    Danced in a skating position with the man's right arm over the woman's shoulder.

    a. L foot heel and back to place.
        R foot toe and back to place.
        R foot heel and back to place.
        L foot heel and kick L across in front of R foot.

    b. Step L, close R, step L.
        Step R, close L, step R.
        Step L, close R, step L.
        Step R, close L, step R.

2. *Black Hawk Waltz* (Black Hawk Waltz)

    Couples stand facing each other holding R hands.

    a. Balance by placing weight on R foot and rasing up and back to place.

        Step on R foot again, and exchange places with your partner, letting her twirl under your arm.

    b. Repeat above four times.

    c. *Crossover step*

        Man—cross R foot over L foot, L over R, R over L, step L, cross R behind L, and point L toe.

        Woman—Same as man, except begin with L foot.

    d. Repeat "c" starting with the other foot.

    e. Repeat "c" and "d."

3. *Put Your Little Foot* (Varsouvienne)

    Danced in same position as Jesse Polka.

    a. Sweep L, step L, close R.
        Sweep L, step L, close R.
        Crossover—sweep L.
        Partners exchange position with three small steps and point R toe.

    b. Repeat above from R side and crossover.

        Repeat both "a" and "b."

c. Chorus—four crossover steps as above without the sweep step close.

4. *Danish Schottische* (Danish Schottische)

Couples use same position as in Jesse Polka.

a. Start with R foot and step, step, step, hop; L foot step, step, step, hop.

b. *Chorus*—step hop, step hop, step hop, step hop.

(Vary the chorus by having both people make small circles to outside or have woman go around man.)

Circle Dances

1. *Seven Jumps* (Seven Jumps)

Formation is a large circle with hands joined—no partners.

a. Skip L seven counts and hop.
   Skip R seven counts and hop.

b. Drop hands, fold arms. On long note, raise R knee, then lower it. Rest on second note.

c. Repeat "a" and "b." Add raise L knee.

d. Repeat "a," "b," and "c." Add kneel on R knee.

e. Repeat "a," "b," "c," and "d." Add kneel on L knee.

f. Continue adding (L elbow on floor, R elbow on floor, chin on floor, etc.).

2. *Come, Let Us Be Joyful* (Come, Let Us Be Joyful)

Formation is a circle of trios with one set facing another, making a small set of six. Preferable to have one man and two women or one woman and two men.

a. *Forward and Bow*—Take three steps forward holding hands, bow, and return to place. Repeat.

b. *Elbow Swing*—Center person links R elbow with person on R and swings around once, then links L elbow with person on L and swings around once. Repeat.

c. *Forward and Pass*—As in "a," advance three steps, bow, and return to place. Advance again but instead of bowing, drop hands and pass R shoulders on to the next trio.

3. *Lili Marlene* (Lili Marlene)

Formation is a double circle of partners with men on the inside.

a. Join L hands, begin on outside foot, and take four steps counterclockwise.

b. Four sliding steps in same direction.

c. Turn around, join inside hands, take four steps, and four slides clockwise as in "a" and "b."

d. *Balance*—Face partner, step on L foot, and swing R foot across front, step on R foot and swing L. Repeat.

e. Link R arms, and walk half around. Link left arms, and walk back to place.

f. *Two Step*—Join inside hands. Begin with inside foot and take step R, slide L, step R. (Women start on L.) Do above action four times, alternating feet.

g. Separate and continue two step in small circles to outside with women moving ahead, and men dropping back to a new partner.

4. *Seven Steps* (Seven Steps)

Formation is a double circle of couples facing counterclockwise, with men inside.

a. *Seven Steps Forward*—Begin on outside foot, and pause on eighth count.

b. *Seven Steps Backward*—Begin on inside foot, and pause on eighth count.

c. *Three Steps Apart*—Release hands, and pause on fourth count.

d. *Three Steps Together*—Pause.

e. *Swing*—Hold R hands high, and run around in place once.

f. *Three Steps Apart*—Pause.

g. *Three Steps Together*—As before, but the man moves forward to a new partner.

h. *Swing*—As before in "e."

Square Dances

1. *Gustav's Skol* (Gustav's Skol)

a. Head couples forward and bow, back to place.

b. Side couples forward and bow, back to place.

c. Repeat "a" and "b."

d. *Chorus*—Side couples form arch by holding inside hands high. Head couples advance, exchange partners, go under arch, and back to place where they swing with an elbow swing.

Head couples arch, and side couples through and swing.

2. *Texas Star* (The Girl I Left Behind Me)

a. Ladies to the center and back to the bar,
    Gents to the center with a right-hand star.

b. The left-hand star, continue and whirl,
    Pass your partner, pick up the next girl.

c. Gents swing out, and the ladies swing in.
    Form that Texas Star ag'in.

d. Gents swing in, ladies swing out,
    Form that Texas Star about.

e. Everybody break and swing,
    Promenade around the ring.

3. *Camptown Races* (Camptown Races)

a. First couple out to the couple at the right, Doodah, Doodah,
    Leave that girl and on to the next, Doodah, Doodah Day,
    Take that girl and on to the next, Doodah, Doodah,
    Leave that girl, go home alone, Doodah, Doodah Day.

b. Forward up six and back,
    Gents do a do-si-do.
    Make that arch and make it high,
    Left hand to lady below.

    (Repeat last part four times till original partners are in place.)

4. *Step Right Back* (Golden Slippers)

a. First couple out and circle four,
    Circle four around the floor.

b. Swing your opposite lady around, Swing her up, and swing her down.

c. Step right back, and watch her smile,
    Step right up, and swing her awhile.
    Step right back, and watch her grin,
    Step right up, and swing her ag'in.

d. Yours is fine, but I'll swing mine any old time.

e. On to the next, and circle four, etc.

f. On to the next, and circle four, etc.

g. Break call . . .

5. *Birdie in the Cage* (Rig-a-Jig-Jig)

a. First couple out and circle four,

Circle four around the floor.

b. Birdie in the cage, close the door,
Circle three around the floor.

c. The bird flew out, the crow hop in,
Look what a handsome thing we have in!

d. The crow hop out, give the birdie a swing,
Both couples swing in a pretty little ring.

e. On to the next, and circle four, etc.

f. On to the next, and circle four, etc.

g. Allemande L your corners all,
A grand R and L around the hall,
Meet your partners all alone,
Pick her up, and promenade home.

Contras

6. *The Virginia Reel* (Irish Washerwoman)

Formation is two straight lines with the gentlemen on the caller's right and the ladies on the left. Should be a minimum of four couples with the gentlemen facing the ladies.

Call: *Forward and back* (8 counts)
Right hand around
Left hand back
Both hands around
Do-si-do
Head couple sashay down the aisle
Sashay back with a great big smile

Reel! Right to your partner, all the way around.
Left to the next, keep moving down.

Head couples sashay back,
Close up lines, don't be slack.

Grand march, lead your lines around,
Take a little walk around the town.

Form an arch and the next couple under,
Come all the way up and go like thunder.

About the Campfire

The "campfire" is a highlight of any resident outdoor education experience and is especially popular the last evening of a program in which students and teachers are away from home and school several days and nights.

When carefully planned and executed, the campfire encourages companionship, unity, and group spirit. It is an event that is usually long remembered with fondness by participants.

The Leader. A person who is able to get every participant's attention upon rising should be designated as the leader. This person should have a quiet manner, be well prepared, and be aware of the sequence of events that are to take place.

The Setting. The leader should view the campfire setting well in advance of the actual event. The setting and location have a bearing upon what can be done. It is important that all those present be able to see the fire, the performers, and the leader.

Opening or Introduction. The opening activity should bring the group together. Perhaps a rowdy song, familiar to everyone, would put everyone in a good mood. This can be followed by an explanation of the meaning of a campfire and what it has meant to others who have experienced it.

Participatory Songs. The use of movements with songs is popular. A favorite song is "My Bonnie Lies over the Ocean," in which the group either rises or sits whenever a word beginning with "B" is encountered. Other favorites include "Ain't No Flies on Me," "Bunny Foo-Foo," and "BINGO."

Skits and Stunts. Skits and stunts are difficult when the group is seated in a circle around the fire. Perhaps it would be better to do them elsewhere when a stage is available. However, if skits are used, they should be well rehearsed, and the adults working with the groups should see to it that "put downs" and "slurs" are avoided. Having all skits focus on a central theme, for example, the history of the site, not only is entertaining but also provides additional learning.

Story Time. Stories can be very special, and depending upon the leader's goals, can be inspirational or hilarious. Obviously the story should be appropriate for the group and can be either "told" or "read." Whether told or read, a soft voice is pleasing and helps prepare children for sleep.

Quiet Songs. It is a good idea to finish the session with quiet songs that the students already know. Music teachers usually delight in teaching children songs that they can use at camp.

Closing. To close, the leader should make some comments about the shared times at camp and then lead a quiet closing song. With careful planning, the groups, one at a time, while still singing, can quietly slip away.

XIV. Water

Children are fascinated about water and water life. This, coupled with the national concern for water resources and the great efforts being made to improve water quality, calls for greater emphasis on the study of rivers, ponds, lakes, marshes, and other bodies of water. Unless children study these resources first-hand, usually as a part of an outdoor education or camping experience, it is doubtful that they will ever really understand or appreciate the importance of these resources.

Water and water resources studies also provide practice and substance for the improvement of data-gathering and observation skills.

The following pages contain several tips, lessons, and guides that teachers have used when involving students in the study of various bodies of water.

Human Impact on Bodies of Water

Much can be learned about a river, lake, or other body of water using the naked eye or a pair of field glasses. Thus, a short field trip along the edge of a river or lake can be beneficial if students know what to look for.

There is usually sufficient evidence present to indicate that people affect water quality.

1. People use the water for transportation (either for economic gain or for leisure). What modes and methods are employed? In what ways have these probably changed over the last 50 to 100 years?

2. People use the water for industrial purposes. What industries are visible along the shoreline that use the water for (1) power, (2) washing purposes, (3) transportation, (4) cooling, and/or (5) disposal of waste?

3. People use the water as a place on which to live. Are there stable houseboats located along the shoreline? Is the water used for drinking or other household purposes? Is there evidence that sewage and rubbish go into the water?

4. The presence of a body of water affects the economic life of the nearby communities. Are "goods" shipped in and out of the area by water-transportation methods? Does the presence of the water attract tourists? If so, what is the attraction? Is the water a barrier to commerce?

5. People are often able to control the water level. Are there dams and spillways present? When were they constructed? Have they permanently changed the body of water? Are they still in use?

6. People's use of bodies of water often results in pollution and the lowering of water quality. What evidence can you find along these lines? What kinds of laws might nearby communities and the state enact to prevent further pollution? What are the natural, social, economic, and political factors which make it difficult to enact laws affecting water quality and use of such bodies of water?

Life in and on a Body of Water

Every body of water contains forms of aquatic life which may be collected, observed, and studied in detail. Any form of life that is collected should be returned unharmed (if at all possible) to where it was found.

Consider these activities when studying the life in a body of water:

1. Use a dip net to collect many organisms that live in the sediments on the bottom of the water. Place all items that are collected in an enamel pan containing a small amount of water, and sort them according to kinds and sizes. If possible, identify the organisms, and ascertain through further study, their physical structures and life habits.

2. Use seines to collect samples of fish life found near the shore. Identify the various types, and study their form and structure. Further investigation will reveal much about them.

3. Gather plankton by seining with an old nylon stocking. Place the material that remains after the water is strained through the stocking in a jar. Use a microscope, and carefully examine the plankton.

4. Search for amphibians which can be found "in" and "out" of the water. Identify the kinds found, and ascertain the environmental factors which contribute to their presence at this particular location.

5. Many kinds of insects live "in," "on," or "above" the water. Collect samples of the "scum," and examine it for insects. Identify the kinds of crawling or flying insects, and find out what they eat and how long they live.

6. Carefully examine submerged rocks and logs for the organisms that are attached.

7. Upon returning to the classroom, classify the organisms you found according to their place in the food chain, their habitat, or their needs. Try to establish a niche or place for each form.

Study of a Spring

These approaches can be employed to study a spring (regardless of its location): (1) discussion using a question-answer format, (2) individual discovery through direct observation, (3) sharing of ideas among individuals, and (4) use of resource materials.

Questions appropriate for use in studying a spring might include the following (teachers and pupils should develop others pertinent to *their own particular spring* and interests):

1.   What is a spring?

2.   How are springs formed? What is the source of the water?

3.   Does this spring have a name? What is the origin of the name?

4.   Is the water safe to drink? Explain.

5.   If the water is contaminated and unsafe for human consumption, what appears to be causing this contamination?

6.   What procedure is used to test water to learn if it is safe to drink?

7.   What is the difference between "safe" drinking water and "contaminated" water?

8.   Are "contaminated water" and "polluted water" synonymous terms? If not, how do they differ?

9.   What is the temperature of the spring water (Celsius/Fahrenheit)? Compare this with the air temperature. Will this relationship hold throughout the year?

10. How much water (liters/gallons) flows from this spring in one minute? How much flows from it in one year? Does it always flow at the same rate?

11. Is there animal life in the water? Carefully examine beneath the leaves and other debris in the water. If any animal life is found, can you identify it?

12. Discuss the "relationship of the spring to other bodies of water in the immediate area." Find out all you can about this relationship.

13. What might be done to improve the quality of water that flows from this spring?

Study of a Pond or Lake

Objectives: To become familiar with a water resource (pond or lake) and explore the related educational potential.

To discover the elements of the aquatic environment.

To discover the impact of people on this water and of the water on humans.

To apply curricular areas such as science, social studies, and mathematics.

1. *Some factors to observe and describe* (set forth your explanations for what you observe):

    a. Color of the water.
    b. Plants along the shore.
    c. Edge between water and land.
    d. Width of the body of water.
    e. Wave action.
    f. Velocity of flow, if any.

    g. Condition of the bottom.
    h. Current flow characteristics.
    i. Materials or scum on the surface.
    j. Signs of animal life.
    k. Signs of human activity.

2. *Ask:* "What factors might be found in, on, or below this body of water for which observational aids may be required if they are to be known?"

    a. *Turbidity:* Secchi disk—or settling test.
    b. *Temperature:* Measure at various depths.
    c. *pH:* Use a piece of litmus test tape.
    d. *Hardness:* Use the soap test, and compare with water from other sources.
    e. *Dissolved oxygen content:* What is the meaning?
    f. *Depth:* Does it vary from place to place and from season to season?

3. *What does it all mean?*

    List the factors you have observed under the categories "abiotic" or "biotic." Which of the biotic factors are producers, consumers, or decomposers?

    Draw lines to connect the factors that are related or interdependent.

    Which of your lines are based upon fact? Which are only hypotheses? Which can be checked by going to authorities or reference materials? Which can be checked through direct observation or experiment?

Study of a River

Objectives: To understand the location, direction of flow, and origin of the river.

To use mathematical skills in determining the width and velocity of the river.

To note how soil erosion is related to river water.

To observe impurities in a river and understand reasons for water purification.

Background information on the river:

1. Which direction does the river flow?

2. Where does the river originate? Where does it end?

3. Through what cities does it pass? Into what larger rivers does it flow?

4. Locate the river on a map, and note its relationship to other important bodies of water, cities, and other points of reference. Plot its route!

Problems related to the river:

1. Measure the river width using the angle method and the Napoleon method.

2. Determine the velocity or rate of current flow.

3. Use a thermometer to find the temperature of the river water, and compare with air temperature. Do this several times a day!

4. Look for evidence to indicate that the water carries soil downstream. Look for evidence to indicate that the river banks are being eroded in some places and that deposition is occurring elsewhere.

Related activities:

1. Do a sedimentation test. Half-fill a jar with sediment from the river bottom, add enough river water to fill the jar, and allow to set. Are layers evident? Repeat using only river water to fill the jar. Does material form at the bottom of the jar?

2. Study a sample of the river water under a microscope.

3. It is said that "river islands slowly flow downstream." Explain!

Studying Water Properties

If one is to understand the functions of water inside a living organism or in our environment, it is necessary to know about some of its physical properties. At the K–3 level, it may be sufficient to introduce concepts such as (1) water is transparent or clear, (2) water occupies space, or (3) water has weight. At the upper-grade levels, however, teachers must introduce many other physical properties.

Preparation: Classroom Introduction and Review	Field Work	Follow-up: Laboratory Investigation
Solubility:		
Transportation of dissolved materials inside plants and animals (circulatory system).	Soil tests for N, P, and K.	Examine tail fin of small fish under microscope.
Transportation of dissolved wastes (city sewage, fertilizer, pesticide, chemical, and industrial wastes).	Sample river, spring, and tap water. Visit sewage plant.	Evaporate water, weigh residues, and examine for composition.
Heat capacity:		
Heating systems in buildings. Circulatory system in mammals distributes heat and cools tissues.	Measure temperature of water at different times.	Make heat capacity experiments.
Perspiration in humans. Transpiration in plants.	Measure plant transpiration using plastic bag.	Weigh transpired water.
Effect of water on climate and weather.	Compare day and night air temperatures near water and inland.	Study maps and graphs of climate and temperature variations.

(Continued)

Preparation: Classroom Introduction and Review	Field Work	Follow-up: Laboratory Investigation
Three states of water:		
Heat energy required to bring about change of state; effects of such changes on weather.	Collect dew. Place plastic bag filled with ice outdoors—note dew formation.	Weigh ice—then water. Measure temperature as ice melts.
Buoyance:		
Transportation on rivers, seas, and lakes.	Use of boats, floats, etc. Dispersal of seeds. Floating plants.	Weight loss experiment. Archimedes principle.
Cohesion and adhesion:		
Capillary action in soil and trees.	See fluid ooze from plants (bulrushes) when cut.	Examine fish tail under microscope. Capillary tube experiment. Celery in dye.
Kinetic energy:		
Water erosion. Generation of electricity. Water wheel in pioneer mills.	Water erosion along shores. Gully and delta formations.	Sand table demonstrations.

Questions

1. How does a large body of water such as the Great Lakes affect the weather and climate of the surrounding area?

2. What is dissolved in tap water?

3. What is carried in solution by river water?

4. How is some of the kinetic energy of the water in a river expended?

5. What advantages does an aquatic habitat have over a terrestrial habitat?

6. Of what significance is water to a plant?

7. In what ways do people use water (internally and externally)?

8. How are crayfish adapted for living in water?

9. How does cell protoplasm utilize water?

10. What is meant by "water pollution"? How is it prevented?

11. What conditions lead to the birth and flow of a spring?

12. Contrast the water requirements of forests with those of prairies or grasslands.

13. Compare primary, secondary, and tertiary water treatments.

14. What forms of pollution are added to rivers by farming? By manufacturing?

A Chart for the Study of Aquatic Life

Life Forms	Where Found										
	Pond						Stream				
	edge	center	shallow	deep	bottom	surface	in pool	in flow	lee of rock	bottom	surface

Collect samples in the field. Examine as many as possible, and return them to the water. Examine microscopic samples in the lab, and return them if possible. Certain forms of life, as well as a diversity of forms, indicate clean water; other forms, along with a lack of diversity, indicate polluted water. Report your findings in the table above. Some life forms to look for:

Plants:

    Algae
    Floating plants
    Rooted plants

Animals:

    Microscopic (sand size)
    Water worms
    Shellfish
    Insects
    Crustaceans
    Fish
    Reptiles and amphibians
    Birds and mammals—as
      temporary residents

Identify a food chain or web based on this information.

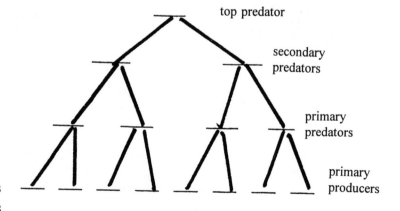

top predator

secondary predators

primary predators

primary producers

A Chart for Testing for Chemicals in Water

Chemicals	Results					
	In Pond		In Stream			
	deep	shallow	above rapids	below rapids	in pool	in flow

A variety of tests can be made to learn if certain chemicals or pollutents are present in the water of streams and ponds. For example, dissolved oxygen is a good indicator of what kinds of fish (or lower animals) may be present. Follow the instructions provided with the test kits, and enter your results in the chart above. Then find out what each means. Combine these results with those you obtained from the aquatic-life survey to obtain a composite picture of the body of water you are studying.

Some chemicals to test for:

Chlorides
Dissolved Oxygen (DO)
Iron
Nitrates
Phosphates
Sulfates

Other tests to run:

Flow (in stream)
Hardness
pH
Suspended Solids
Temperature
Total Dissolved Solids

XV. Weather

We cannot escape from the weather. It surrounds us when we step outdoors, and affects our daily moods, behaviors, and activities. It determines what we can and cannot do, and places a damper on many a field trip, ball game, picnic, and boat ride.

We read about the weather in the newspapers and see or hear reports and predictions on television and radio everyday. It is of interest to everyone, and comments about weather conditions are usually a part of the exchange of greetings that take place when friends meet. We even have a "Weather TV Channel."

First-hand study of weather affords great opportunities for learners to gather data using a variety of instruments, to record and interpret these data, to make predictions about the future, and to soon learn if they were accurate.

The "weather activities" that follow have been helpful to teachers and other outdoor leaders when working with children in their weather studies.

Use Weather to Teach Children to
Observe, Record, and Predict

Although "weather" is the subject of many school and camp instructional units, teachers and campers rarely utilize local weather conditions as effectively as they might in their programs. Here is a readily available and natural resource that can be used for observation, data-gathering, involvement, and predictive experiences.

Local weather conditions are useful for investigation because:

1. Weather consist of phenomena to be observed and measured—temperature, barometric pressure, precipitation, wind direction and speed, relative humidity, cloud type, and cover.

2. Weather conditions change from hour-to-hour and day-to-day, thereby providing variety in the observations and the data recorded. These conditions often appear to be related; at other times they appear unrelated.

3. Some conditions such as barometric pressure and temperature can be readily observed and measured; while others such as cloud type and cover are less subject to measurement, and observers have to make interpretive judgments when recording conditions.

4. Children can be actively involved in observing, measuring, and recording weather data. They can position and read some instruments and manipulate others.

5. Students can convert the data recorded on an hourly or daily basis to long-term generalizations about weather, graph construction, basic statistics, and the like.

6. Pupils' predictions are put to the test within a short time.

7. Children can feel and directly experience the conditions they measure.

8. Apparatus and instruments are relatively inexpensive, easy to use, and require little storage space.

A group of children might wish to investigate problems or studies such as:

1. Recording weather conditions on the school or camp grounds over an extended period of time and comparing them with conditions reported at an official weather station nearby.

2. Making comparisons between conditions at various points on the site.

3. Determining the effect of weather conditions on humans. (Is temperature the only factor that makes us feel cold?)

4. Interpreting what people *really mean* when they use terms such as "nice day" and "stormy day" and "miserable day."

5. Determining which month (or week) of the year has the most or the least variable weather.

6. Identifying and testing relationships between weather and other factors such as the activity of insects and birds, the operation of the heating plant, inside relative humidity, or the way people dress.

Obviously, questions will arise and be the basis for additional first-hand investigations. Subsequently, students will have to use many other research techniques and may want to construct graphs or use other methods to clarify, depict, and interpret their data.

Groups undertaking weather studies should have their own "kits" of instruments so that their observations can be made without interference and so that instruments are available when they are needed. Such kits should include (1) an aneroid barometer, (2) inexpensive psychrometers, (3) inexpensive household thermometers, (4) wind-speed and direction indicators, and (5) reference materials such as relative humidity tables, Beaufort wind scales, cloud charts, and data-recording sheets.

These instruments can be purchased for about $35. Since children often mishandle instruments, relatively inexpensive hardware store items usually serve as well as expensive scientific items. Classroom-constructed apparatus will often suffice.

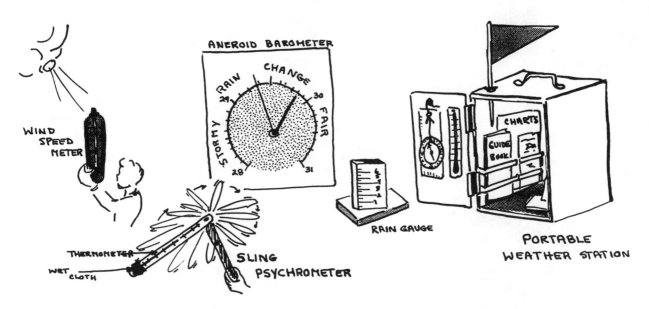

Fixed *indoor* weather stations are being installed by some schools and camps so that outside conditions can be measured without going outdoors. These inherently remove much of the activity or pupil involvement from the process. Pupils do not experience the conditions they measure or study. There *is a difference* between standing indoors and recording data about a cold wintry blizzard and going outdoors in the storm. *Children should directly experience weather phenomena as they measure.* Thereby, teaching objectives in the affective domain are more likely to be attained!

Weather Exploration

Objectives: To help students:

Learn about some of the basic weather factors and how to measure them.

Discover some of the weather components.

Develop some simple weather instruments.

Become acquainted with appropriate observation, data-gathering, and interpretive techniques.

1. Introduce students to phenomena commonly measured in the study of weather.

   a. What are some basic weather elements? Define the following, and explain their relationship to the other elements:

(1)	Wind	(5)	Clouds
(2)	High pressure	(6)	Temperature
(3)	Low pressure	(7)	Air mass
(4)	Humidity (relative)	(8)	Cold front, warm front

   b. On the basis of these definitions and observations, work with students in making some simple instruments to measure some weather components:

   (1) Wind vane: feather in cork or cardboard vane.

   (2) Bottle with balloon and pointer: What does this measure?

   (3) Wet- and dry-bulb thermometers.

   (4) Beaufort scale for wind speed.

   c. Explain and demonstrate the use of the "homemade" instruments. Point out the advantages and the limitations.

   d. Demonstrate the use of purchased instruments found in the weather "kit" or "station."

2. Deal with some of the considerations necessary in making weather predictions. Consult the following section, "Weather Forecasting Information," along with current weather maps.

3. Establish a list of weather conditions which you can observe now. Use the instruments available to you to gather appropriate data and to make the observations. Interpret your data.

4. On the basis of these data, make predictions about what is likely to happen weatherwise in the next 24 hours.

Weather Forecasting Information

Observers forecast the weather using their own observations in conjunction with preceding weather reports. Forecasts are often based on relationships such as the following (gathered from various sources):

1. A falling barometer indicates an approaching "low" with a storm.

2. A rising barometer indicates the passing of the "low" and the approach of a "high" and fair weather.

3. The passing of a "low" in summer will be followed by warmer weather.

4. The passing of a "low" in winter will be followed by colder weather, perhaps with a "cold front" from the Far North and with blizzards in regions east of the Far West.

5. Winds from the east or northeast foretell a "low" coming from the west with its center to the north of the observer, with rain to come within 24 hours.

6. Winds from the east or northeast foretell a "low" coming from the west with its center to the west or to the south of the observer, often with heavy, chilly rain, and cold weather.

7. Winds swinging from the southeast to the southwest indicate that the center of the "low" has passed to the east and that fair and colder weather will soon follow.

8. Winds swinging from the east or northeast to the northwest also indicate that the center of the "low" has passed to the east and that fair and colder weather will soon follow.

9. Cirrus and cirrostratus clouds, coming from the west with a gray sky, indicate the approach of a "low" with a storm.

10. A bright blue sky with cirrus wisps and the wind in the west or northwest will be followed by fair weather for 24 to 48 hours.

11. A bright blue sky with numerous cumulus clouds may be followed by stratocumulus and rain or snow flurries during the middle of the day and early afternoon, but by sunset, the sky may be fair.

12. If the lightning of a thunderstorm appears to the northwest, west, or southwest, the thunderstorm will come nearer the observer and perhaps pass overhead.

13. If in fall or spring the temperature falls to 4 degrees Celsius (40 degrees Fahrenheit) or so at the end of a clear, calm day, one may expect frost in low places by morning. Frost will likely not form if clouds cover the sky or the wind blows during the night.

Collecting Weather Information

Objectives: To learn if weather conditions are the same at all points of the school site or camp area.

To learn if changes occur simultaneously at different locations.

To identify relationships among weather elements.

To analyze recorded information and generalize from the specific observations.

Equipment: A kit of weather instruments, a weather conditions record sheet (see next page), a
(for group reference on weather, and a set of weather information sheets.
of 3 or 4)

Procedure: The class should be divided into groups (teams) of three or four students each. Each team should select an observational site some distance from any other team and make observations over a period of several days at selected times, such as 7:00 A.M., 10:00 A.M., 12:30 P.M., 3:00 P.M., etc.

When all teams have completed their observations, they should resume their studies as a class, discuss their findings, and answer such questions as:

1. When and where were the highest and lowest temperatures recorded? What was the mean temperature?

2. What was the greatest wind velocity recorded?

3. What was the range of barometric pressures? What was the mean barometric pressure?

4. What adjectives were used? How many were used?

5. What relationships were noted? Can we generalize?

Weather Conditions Record Sheet

Location of Station _____   Date _____   Team Members _____, _____, _____

	1	2	3	4	5	6	7	8
Time of Day								
Temperature (at 1 m/3 ft.)								
Temperature (at Surface)								
Wind Direction								
Wind Velocity								
Barometric Pressure								
Relative Humidity								
Precipitation (Rain, Snow)								
Clouds (Type and Cover)								
Adjectives (Describing Weather)								

Microclimates: A Lesson on Temperature Variation

This activity is designed for use as part of a weather unit. When students obtain data from their own weather station or from the news media, they should recognize that not all points in an area have the same conditions. *Some places are warmer or colder than others!*

A microclimatic study using temperature may demonstrate that great differences exist in relatively small areas (as small as a hectare/acre or even within a radius of a few meters/feet). On one school site, children obtained temperature readings ranging from 16 to 51 degrees Celsius (60 to 124 degrees Fahrenheit) when the air temperature was 31 degrees Celsius (88 degrees Fahrenheit).

Obtaining Temperatures:

Look for different surface materials and textures or open exposed areas and sheltered areas, and measure the temperature of each. Look for holes in trees or in the ground. Take temperatures at the surface above grass, blacktop, gravel, concrete, wood, etc. Compare temperatures on different slopes and on the various sides of the building. Check the temperatures at the base of a tree, in the lower branches, and at the tip of the outer branches.

Take readings throughout the day. Take them over a period of several days, and notice the effect of general weather conditions and season on the temperature ranges. Are they as great on cloudy days as on sunny days?

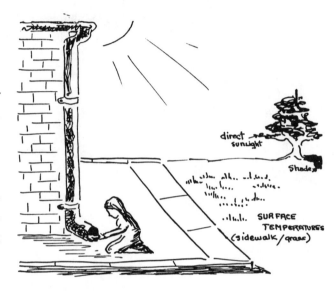

Significance of the Temperature Variations:

The information collected about temperature variations can be used to bring about some appreciation of the effect of weather on plants and animals. Study the forms of life found in the various areas. Are they similar? Are the plants found in open sunny spots of the same species as those found in the shade? Under what conditions is the greatest variety found? Where do you find the greatest quantity of plants? How does temperature affect animal activity? Where do different animals go during cold days? Where can they be found on hot days? Compare with human behaviors.

XVI. Winter Studies

Study outdoors in the winter when it is cold and the ground is covered with snow? Absolutely!

Studies in the outdoors in winter can be enjoyable, highly educational, and rewarding. Unfortunately, many teachers avoid such studies, since they lack guidelines for them. This section provides those guidelines.

Activities contained in other sections of *Tips and Tricks,* for example, animal tracking, insects in winter, and birds (all in Section II), twigs in winter (Section XII), and weather (Section XV), can all be done during the winter.

While this section includes some similar activities, it deals primarily with those that can only be done in the winter when snow and ice are present.

Comfort in the Snow and Cold

Children do not always realize the relationship between their own comfort and their dress as they prepare for outdoor activity in cold weather. It is very difficult to concentrate when your feet or fingers are cold!

Among the greatest health hazards in winter are frostbite, hypothermia, and snow blindness. You should be aware of these problems and know how to solve them. If students are dressed warmly, outdoor activities in winter can be healthy and invigorating.

Impress upon your students the need to dress well for winter. Deal with the advantages of using layered clothing of good insulating material, such as wool. Caps and hoods are very important. (About half of a person's body heat loss is through the head.) Impress upon your students the need to wear warm footgear that will accommodate several pairs of warm socks. Mittens keep hands warmer than gloves.

Becoming Acclimatized to Snow:

1. Breathe in cold air. Describe your reactions to it.

2. Feel snow crystals. Describe their shapes.

3. Feel the snow. Is it cold? Observe, and describe how your hand feels. What color is it? Is there steam coming from it? Are there things other than snow that feel colder?

4. Compare the feel of snow with the feel of other cold objects, such as wood, concrete, metal, a tree, and glass. Describe the differences.

   > Don't touch cold metal with a wet tongue!

5. Taste newly fallen snow. Why do we not use it instead of water? Point out reasons for not eating "unmelted snow"!

Snow Study Introduction

Winter Color:

We usually think of snow as white. On a walk on the school site or in a nearby park, look for other shades of colors. Using pastels or crayons, sketch a picture of the landscape in the late afternoon or early morning. How many colors or shades of colors can you find in the snow?

Snow Names:

How many kinds of snow can you find? Some of the most commonly recognized include:

Falling snow	Drifted snow
Fallen snow	Crusty snow

How many more can you identify? List as many kinds of snow as you can think of. Invent words that seem appropriate. (Eskimos have over a dozen different words for snow.)

Simulated Snow Drifts:

Make your own drifts. Use a pan for the earth, salt for snow, and various objects (forks, sticks, jars, stones, etc.) for obstructions. Shake salt over the "earth," then carefully blow the snow into drifts, around obstructions, etc. record what happens. Sketches will help.

How do the "obstructions" affect the shape of the drifts?_____

_____

Where do the drifts form?_____

_____

What "patterns" or "designs" are evident in the drifts?_____

_____

(Go outdoors, find similar snow formations, and sketch them. Where do they occur?)

Snow Melt

Color and Snow Melt:

On a *sunny* day, place different colored sheets of construction paper on the snow where each will receive equal amounts of sunlight during the day. Place them out of the wind, or weight them carefully. At regular intervals, measure and record how deeply each has melted into the snow. List the colors in order according to rate of heat absorption. How might this relate to our choice of clothing color for various seasons?

Depth of Melt for Colors

Time	Red	Yellow	Blue	Brown	Black	Green	Other

Salt and Snow Melt:

Fill two cans with loosely packed snow. Label them "A" and "B." Add a handful of salt to can "A." At regular intervals, observe the melting condition and temperatures. Record. Based on your results, explain why salt is spread on icy roads.

	Can "A"		Can "B"	
Time	Temperature	Condition	Temperature	Condition

Snowflakes

Collect falling snow on a dark piece of cloth (your coat sleeve will do) or a dark piece of paper. Examine a good snowflake with a hand lens, and quickly sketch it. Do this with several snowflakes.

Are they all alike? _____

How many sides do they have? _____

Compare the shapes found with the diagrams on the "International Classification of Snow Crystals," which appears below.

Examine and sketch old snow crystals. Are they the same as, or different from, newly fallen snow?

Describe: _____

_____

Catch and examine some snowflakes at the beginning of a snowfall, during its height, and at the end. Do their shapes remain the same during the entire snowfall, or do they change?

Describe: _____

_____

International Classification of Snow Crystals

Aging Snow

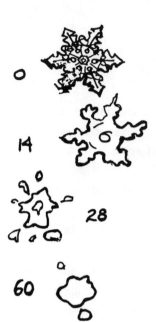

Melting Snow Crystals:

As snowflakes melt, they tend toward a spherical shape. This is called destructive metamorphism of snow crystals. To observe this, examine and sketch the shape of a snowflake as soon as it has fallen (a hand lens will be helpful). Continue to sketch as it melts. Several flakes may be observed and sketched.

What happens to the shape of the crystals as they

melt? _____

_____

What happens to their sharp edges? _____

_____

Demonstration of Melting Crystals:

On a smooth, non-porous surface, use a medicine dropper of water to make a "snowflake" about 3 centimeters (1³⁄₁₆ inches) in diameter.

First drop the ends of the six sides:

Continue to fill in until some of the drops come together:

Do this until all of the drops are touching. What has happened to the shape of the "flake?"

_____

(It should have changed from a six-sided form to a spherical one.)

Exploring a Snowdrift

Profile of a Snowdrift:

Find a deep natural drift. Using a shovel or a piece of plywood, carefully slice through the drift to the ground. Carefully examine, and measure the layers. Record the following information:

1. How many layers are present? _____

2. What is the depth of each layer? _____

    _____

3. What colors are found in each layer? _____

    _____

4. Feel the layers. In what ways do they differ in hardness, iciness, grittiness, etc.?

    _____

5. How do the crystals in the various layers differ in size and shape? _____

    _____

Temperatures in the Snowdrift:

Snow can act as an insulating blanket. To demonstrate this, take and record temperatures of:

Air: _____

Very top of drift: _____

Halfway through drift: _____

Under snow at ground level: _____

Chart your results!

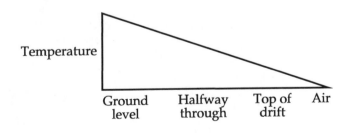

NOTE: During a "cold spell," your chart should look like the one illustrated here.

Make a Snow Shelter:

A temporary snow shelter (quin zhee) in which a person can enjoy the feeling of living under snow can easily be built.

To make a quin zhee, build a pile of snow as deep as possible, and allow it to set for a few hours. Then, carefully dig out the shelter, leaving a shell about 15 to 40 centimeters (about 6 to 16 inches) thick.

The floor should be ground level. This will facilitate heat flow from the soil into the shelter. A plastic sheet can be used to cover the floor. Block the door with cakes of snow overnight, and make vent holes in the top and near the floor to facilitate ventilation.

The quin zhee will act as an insulator from the outside environment. Once built, it can serve as a temporary shelter and for sleeping outdoors.

> **CAUTION:** The quin zhee should be used only under adult supervision. If there should be an excessive amount of snow overhead, it could develop into a very dangerous situation. The quin zhee could collapse, resulting in the suffocation of anyone inside.

Snow Density

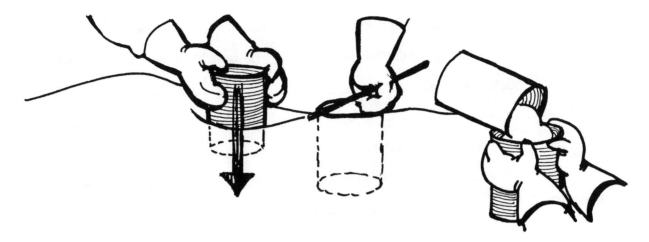

Snow density varies according to depth and age conditions, snow, air temperature, and wind. To measure snow density, collect snow from several locations under various conditions.

1. Collect four samples of snow: freshly fallen snow, snow that fell several days ago, snow from a drift, snow that has been plowed into a drift, snow that has been walked on, etc.

   a. Collect your samples of snow by using a large can, such as a fruit juice can, with both ends removed. Carefully press the full length of the can into the snow without compacting it. Using a wooden paddle, slice the snow from the ends of the can so that it is level.

   b. Label four cans (also fruit juice cans) that have had only one end removed. Label them "A," "B," "C," and "D."

   c. Transfer each sample of snow to its own can.

2. Bring the cans of snow samples indoors, and allow the snow to melt.

3. After the snow has melted, measure the depth of water in each can.

4. For each sample, divide the depth of the snow by the depth of the water in each can to find the snow to water ratio.

5. Record the ratio of snow to water for each sample.

   Sample "A" _____   Sample "B" _____   Sample "C" _____   Sample "D" _____

6. If the ratio is not constant, explain the differences: _____

   _____

Icicles

1. *Find a building with icicles. After exploration, answer these questions:*

   a. What is the age of the building? _____ How might the building's age affect
      icicle formation? _____

   b. Of what color and material is the roof? _____
      How might these affect icicle formation? _____

   c. On which side of the building are the most icicles? _____
      Explain: _____

2. *Measuring the icicles. Find and record for the icicles indicated:*

	Longest Icicle	**Thickest Icicle**	**Thinnest Icicle**
Length	_____	_____	_____
Base Circumference	_____	_____	_____
Ratio Length to Base	_____	_____	_____
Where Found	_____	_____	_____

   a. Are the ratios the same for all icicles? _____ Explain:_____
      _____

   b. What did you find to suggest that the wind affects icicle formation? _____

3. *Break an icicle, and, using a hand lens, observe the layers of ice.*

   How do the icicles form? _____

4. *Checking for impurities or sediments.*

   Melt an icicle, and pour the water through filter paper (coffee filters work well). Using
   a hand lens, examine what is left in the filter.

   a. Describe: _____

   b. Does this say anything about why we should or should not eat icicles? _____
      _____

Aquatic Explorations in Winter

Ice Observations:

Chop a hole through the ice cover of a pond. Remove chips of ice from various depths, and take indoors.

> **CAUTION:** Exercise great care before stepping onto any ice-covered pond or water. Be certain that it will support your weight and that you do not slip in!

1. How thick is the ice? _____

2. Describe its texture: _____

3. Did you find several "kinds" of ice? If so, describe the ice types, and tell where they were found: _____

    _____

4. Explain why the ice that forms from a pond is dark and why the slush that forms from ice is white: _____

    _____

5. Measure and record the temperature of the water under the ice:_____

Organisms in the Ice Water:

1. Collect a jar of water, and examine it indoors. What organisms do you find? _____

    _____

2. Examine the melted ice chips. Are there any organisms in them?_____

    Describe them: _____

Follow-up:

Keep the water in tightly covered jars in a sunny window. Observe and record organisms as they appear. This observation can continue for months, provided the jars are kept tightly covered.

Mini-explorations

Plants. Choose a rectangular plot of snow-covered ground for this exploration. (One meter [three feet] is sufficient.) Mark the plot, and remove the snow, being careful not to disturb what is underneath.

1. Look for green plants that are still "alive" during the winter. Carefully record the size of each, and sketch it. Count the number in the plot. Take a photograph if possible. When finished, replace the snow.

2. Try to identify the sketches. Predict what the plants will look like during the growing season.

3. When spring comes, return to the plot, and find the plants again. Observe them during the growing season. Were your predictions correct?

Animal Habitats. Look in the ground, in wood piles, under the bark of dead trees, in rotting wood, and at the bases of buildings for small animals. Many of them will be insects or other arthropods, but some will be small mammals, such as field mice. Record what you find:

Place	Animals

Soil Temperatures. If the soil can be penetrated with a soil thermometer, measure and record:

| Time of Day | Location | Temperature | | | Arthropods Present |
		3 cm	10 cm	20 cm	

Trees in Winter

Tree Shapes (Contour Drawing)

First, look at something, for example, a building. Follow its outline in the air with your hand. Next, follow its outline on a piece of paper with your finger (without looking at the paper). Finally, use a crayon and follow its outline on the paper (still without looking at the paper).

Using this technique, boldly draw the main outlines of several trees. Look at the outlines. In what ways do they differ? This is a good way to identify trees in winter.

Tree Bark

Using a crayon or soft pencil, make rubbings of several trees. How do they differ? This is another way to identify trees in the winter.

NOTE: Refer to Section XI, "Nature Arts and Crafts," and Section XII, "Plants," for additional hints.

Tree Buds

During the summer, trees and other plants make use of solar energy to produce the food used by all living things. They do something else that is amazing—they produce buds from which the next year's leaves and flowers develop.

Select one large bud from a tree or shrub (lilacs are best). Very carefully dissect the bud. Remove one layer at a time, and line the layers up in rows. Use a hand lens to examine the pieces of the bud. Sketch and describe them.

What do you see? What shapes do the pieces have? (They should look like small leaves of the plant.) *Is there anything in the center of the very large buds?* (These may be flower buds.) *What is covering the bud?* (Usually waxy or fuzzy coats prevent water loss from the bud.)

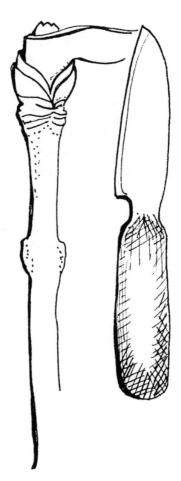

Winter Birds

It is probably more enjoyable to watch birds in winter than in any other season. Then they are hungry, bold, and will come to your feeder, where you can observe them. In addition, there are usually fewer species in winter to observe and to confuse the beginning bird watcher.

The Bird Feeder:

1. Set out a variety of bird food, such as sunflower seeds, commercial mix, cracked corn, suet, bread crumbs, orange slices, bread soaked in grease, or any others that you know birds will eat.

2. Observe and record:

    Food: Which birds eat what food?

    Manner of eating: Which birds eat alone? In groups?
    Which birds eat while clinging? Perching? On the ground?
    Which birds are greedy? Messy? Fussy?
    Which birds are timid? Bold?

A Winter Bird Clue Chart:

Based on what you see at the feeder, develop a winter bird clue chart, modeled after the one on page 24.

Winter Bird Counts:

Contact a member of a local Audubon Society or bird club to learn what is being done in your area about the annual Audubon Christmas count. Perhaps you can learn what kinds of birds were discovered in your community. Perhaps you can help take the count next year.

XVII. Environmental Values

Most educators believe that environmental values are learned throughout our lifetime and, therefore, can be taught. Environmental values are positive statements about the care and condition of the environment that can be acted upon by the person stating the preference. For example, if we value putting a campfire out to prevent the forest from burning, in most cases, we will act upon this value and extinguish the campfire when we leave.

Teachers have a responsibility to parents and the community to teach certain agreed-upon environmental values to students. Examples of environmental values issues that are generally agreed upon are:

1. Most endangered plants and animals should be protected.

2. Litter should be picked up and properly disposed of in receptacles.

3. Private property should be respected and avoided, unless permission is given to be there.

4. Items carried into the woods and fields should be carried out.

5. Most native plant species should be treated with respect.

6. Trails should be used for hiking whenever possible.

7. Campfires should be properly confined and kept small.

8. Fish and game laws should be understood and followed.

9. Recycling paper, glass, and plastic is a good idea.

Students can learn about environmental values through lessons in the outdoors. In order to do this, the leader must be able to state the value or values to be taught and learned.

Instructors need to be aware of particular values that the school and community want students to develop. When these are listed and lessons are planned so they can be learned, teachers can usually avoid criticism for attempting to teach these values.

Other environmental values that do not have the support of the school and community should not be approached in the same way. Dealing with these controversial issues requires a different teaching strategy. For example, the use of nuclear energy to generate electricity is a controversial topic. This issue should be researched and discussed, and the students should be encouraged to reach their own conclusions. The teacher's role in dealing with these unresolved and complicated issues should be one of providing the classroom climate necessary to examine and debate the values involved. Teachers may share their own values position on an issue only after the students have had opportunities to arrive at their own values choices.

Some controversial environmental values issues are:

1. Government restricting the use of privately owned wetlands.

2. Methods for disposing of solid wastes.

3. Using certain pesticides and deciding how much of the residue on food is safe.

4. Cutting old-growth forests.

5. Converting rain forests to pasture land for beef production.

6. Using energy efficient light bulbs and fuels.

7. Developing solar energy systems.

8. Using ethanol in gasoline.

9. Grazing sheep and cattle on public lands.

10. Restricting the number of people allowed in state and national parks.

11. Converting open land to housing or industrial development.

12. Keeping certain animals in circuses and zoos.

13. Manufacturing and selling throw-away utensils, batteries, razors, pens, and other convenience items.

14. Protecting certain predators such as wolves and grizzly bears in areas near people.

15. Hunting, trapping, and fishing as threats to animal populations.

The task of deciding which environmental values are generally agreed upon by the community and which are potentially controversial is sometimes difficult. Instructors may find that listing environmental values in two columns can help them determine how to approach each lesson. When they are clear about the two main types of environmental values and how to conduct lessons for each one, they usually avoid most of the pitfalls of values education.

Every environmental issue is potentially controversial to some degree. For example, some parents may object to children participating in a litter pick up because of the safety and health hazards involved. By keeping the communication lines open among administrators, board members, and parents, instructors can successfully teach about environmental values outdoors and indoors.

The following lessons focus upon teaching and learning environmental values.

Environmental Values: What Should I Do?

Anticipatory Set: A person's lifestyle is composed of a set of behaviors determined in part by our values. In the area of environmental values, we are faced with many choices such as:

1. Should we use paper napkins at meals or not use them because trees must be cut to make napkins?

2. Should we buy drinks in recyclable containers or in containers that are difficult to recycle?

3. Should we establish a prairie ecosystem or let "nature take its course" and allow trees to grow up in the prairie area and eventually kill the prairie grasses?

4. Should we keep people out of certain outdoor areas to maintain them as "natural areas" or let people use these areas even though they will be changed by human impact?

5. Should we remove stray cats from the area to protect birds and other small animals, or should we allow the cats to roam free and eat what they want?

Objectives: 1. To practice making ethical decisions about specific environmental issues.

2. To identify the reasons and values behind our environmental choices after discussing the issues.

3. To attempt to determine how our past experiences may have contributed to forming our values about the environment.

Introduction: Ethical decisions can result from investigating issues and deciding upon the proper actions to take. The process usually begins by asking the question "What should I do in this situation?" Environmental ethics involve choosing what is right and good as we use the earth's resources to live and survive. Our personal values influence how we answer the question of how to use resources. The following activities will help you explore ethical decision making, personal values, and how our experiences shaped them.

Development: The class is divided into small groups of three or four people. The members of each group select several environmental values activities to do. After completing each activity, they will discuss their preferred solution, state their reasons for choosing it, list the important underlying values, and try to determine how their experiences might have helped to form these values. The purpose of the discussions is not to try to influence others to conform to their values, but to identify similarities and differences in the choices, reasons, values, and experiences. Each group will select a recorder to report on some of the interesting results of the discussions.

Activities:

1. Find a tree or other plant that you consider to be useful for a craft project, and decide whether or not you would cut it down to make the item.

2. Search for something that you consider to be visual pollution and would like to eliminate. (Be creative and pretend that you had the power to remove whatever you didn't like.) What would you get rid of? Why?

3. Search the area to find something you value for some reason. Then either bring it back or make a drawing of it to share. State your reason for selecting what you did.

4. Find some object or event in the environment that makes the biggest impact on other living things . . . the smallest impact on other living things.

5. Identify at least five different birds, and then rank them according to which you like the most to which you like the least. Try to figure out the values behind each person's selections.

Reflecting on the Experience:

1. What activity generated the most discussion?

2. What activity generated the greatest value conflicts? . . . the most agreement?

3. Were you able to trace the formation of some values to a specific set of experiences or experience? Explain.

4. Would more information about a particular issue have helped you decide what choice is more ethical? Explain.

5. Were you tempted to try to change the values of others in your group? Explain.

6. What is the proper role of a teacher in dealing with environmental ethics and values with students?

Leave Only Footprints

Value: People who use the land for recreation should consider others who use the land and leave nothing more than footprints behind.

Objectives: To prepare the students to:

Orally explain the meaning and importance of the terms "no-trace," "consumptive," and "non-consumptive" land use.

Orally explain several ways in which people leave evidence of their presence on public land.

Compare and contrast the types of evidence found in two specific locations. (At least three similarities should be noted.)

Introduction and Preparation: No-trace and non-consumptive land uses are values that some people practice in public recreation areas because they believe that all people have a right to use the land for enjoyment and that they should not alter its natural state. No-trace use means that no significant evidence of human activity will remain on the land. Non-consumptive use results in very little loss or reduction of natural resources from the land. Some examples of non-consumptive uses are hiking, swimming, bird watching, picnicking, and photography. Consumptive uses result in the loss or reduction of natural resources. Some examples of consumptive uses are burning wood, chopping down a tree, disturbing the soil, or picking a flower.

Activity: Have the participants form a line and survey two adjacent areas receiving different land uses. Ask them to note evidence of human use and, when possible, to collect some of the evidence in plastic bags. Instruct them to make notes on a data collection sheet similar to the one presented on the following page in order to list and classify the evidence of human use of the land.

Human Evidence Data Collection Sheet

Evidence Found	Possible Human Activity	Use (Check One)	
		Consumptive	Non-consumptive

Resources Needed: Data collection sheet, pen or pencil, clipboard, bags.

Procedure: Have the students pair up, form a long line (outstretched arm-length distance apart), and alternately count off one and two.

Have them walk over the land. Instruct the number one's to record the findings on the data collection sheet, and instruct the number two's to collect the evidence of human use in the bags.

When they are finished, have them return to the meeting area, analyze the results, and then report the findings to the group.

Evaluation: Have partners in each pair test each other on the first two objectives.

Ask each student to write a paragraph comparing and contrasting the survey examples of human evidence found in the two public areas.

Bibliography: Waterman, Laura and Guy. *Backwoods Ethics*. Washington, D.C.: Stone Wall Press Inc. 1980.

Reflecting on the Experience:

1. From the evidence of how people use the land, can you make some statements about what they value and what they don't?

2. What values seem to be of higher priority than no-trace or non-consumptive values, judging from the evidence found?

Making a Personal Outdoor Values Inventory

Introduction: Do you have a favorite season of the year? If so, you probably like that season because you value some things you can do outdoors then. If choosing one favorite season is difficult, you may enjoy being outdoors all year round. Completing this inventory may help you to explore some of your values about the present season.

1.   Go outdoors, and locate a beautiful

   Sight _____   Sound _____

   Texture _____   Smell _____

2.   Go outdoors, and find a place where you feel peaceful and relaxed. Describe:

   _____

   _____

   _____

3.   List three early memories of the outdoors at this time of year:

   _____

   _____

   _____

4.   If this season were like an animal, what would it be? _____

5.   List four outdoor activities you like to do best during this season:

   _____

   _____

   _____

   _____

6.   List at least two outdoor activities you want to do this season but haven't done for a while:

   _____

   _____

7. List the evidence found of a situation in which the values of a few human beings have had an effect on other human beings:

_____

_____

_____

_____

8. Make friends with this season. Describe your new friend, using a story or a poem:

_____

_____

_____

_____

_____

_____

9. Find a beautiful natural object. Describe it in detail:

_____

_____

_____

_____

10. Find things outdoors that make you feel

Angry _____   Afraid _____

Sad _____   Happy _____

11. Find a good change that has taken place recently. Describe it:

_____

_____

_____

12. During this time of year I like the following things:

Yes ☐   No ☐ Wind _____

Yes ☐   No ☐ Rain _____

Yes ☐   No ☐ Snow _____

Yes ☐   No ☐ Hail _____

Yes ☐   No ☐ Sunshine _____

Yes ☐   No ☐ Clouds _____

Yes ☐   No ☐ Present temperature _____

Yes ☐   No ☐ Other _____

13. Provide five words that best describe this season:

    _____

14. On a scale similar to the one below, indicate how much you value this season by placing an "X" on the line.

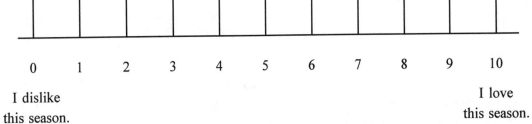

    0   1   2   3   4   5   6   7   8   9   10

I dislike   I love

this season.   this season.

Reflecting on
the Experience:

1. Did you become more aware of what you value about this present season?

2. What past experiences might account for your present values?

Litter

Littering is usually caused by people who don't value a clean environment and is usually considered an eyesore to others. Litter often causes problems for animals and often necessitates costly clean-up programs.

Litter Lines:

1. Ask each participant to go outside and find five pieces of different types of litter, such as metal, paper, or plastic. When all of them return, ask each person to find a partner and place the pieces of litter in a line from the most offensive to the least offensive. If a disagreement arises about where an item belongs on the line, let the partners discuss the reasons and attempt to reach an agreement. After all 10 items are lined up, have each pair share results with the rest of the group.

2. Encourage discussion about the placement of the pieces of litter.

3. Then ask the partners to rearrange their 10 pieces of litter according to the following:

    a. Most abundant resource to the least abundant.
    b. Largest to the smallest.
    c. Most visible to the least visible.
    d. Most harmful to the least harmful.
    e. Most biodegradable to the least biodegradable.

4. Ask the partners to make guesses about the values and lifestyles of those who littered.

Litter and Its Setting:

The setting often affects the way we see and value things. For example, one piece of litter along a forest path stands out, and many of us don't like to see it. On the other hand, a city street cluttered with litter is often taken for granted.

1. Have the students take a survey of an outdoor area and use a chart, such as the one following, for recording information about what they see and how much they value it. Advise them to pay special attention to such objects as signs, utility poles, buildings, sidewalks, plants, leaves, rocks, lights, evidence of vandalism, and other things that may be found in both types of settings and to be aware of events such as wind, temperature, sounds, and movements.

2. After they complete the survey in one location, have them go to another (preferably in a different type of area) and repeat the process. Ask them to compare the results of each survey to determine if the setting or context affects their awareness and their evaluation of things.

Outdoor Area Surveyed: _____

Object or Event	How Valued (On scale 1 – 10) (10 is high)	Reason/Explanation

Reflecting on the Experience:

1. What did you learn about awareness and what you valued?

2. Did you value the same objects or events differently because of the settings in which you found them?

3. Did you notice a certain object or event better because of the setting in which you found it?

4. Did you behave differently because of the setting? In what ways?

5. Do you want to change the way you value certain objects or events? If so, in what way?

Other Values Activities

The following activities are designed to help students to understand their own and other people's environmental values.

How Would a Rabbit See the World?:

We usually see the world from the standpoint of our own values and needs. A rabbit would see the tender grass and other edible plants as food and would see a brush pile as a place of shelter to hide from enemies. A bird might see the seeds on plants and the places to perch.

People also see the world from their own perspectives. Artists see places to paint or sketch and notice patterns and colors. Foresters see trees and consider the timber that might be cut from them.

Pretend that you are different wildlife species and people, and walk around and see the world through their eyes. Some interesting people to role play might be an architect, a teacher, a hunter, a farmer, a building contractor, a nature lover, a realtor, and a scientist.

Reflecting on the Experience:

1. What were the different wildlife species and people chosen to role play?

2. Which ones created the most interest and insight? What others could be added if this activity were repeated?

3. Are the students now better able to empathize with environmental values other than their own?

Value Tags:

1. Ask your instructor to give you eight shipping tags containing different "values" words, for example, (1) beautiful, (2) useful, (3) valuable, (4) artistic, (5) good, (6) gentle, (7) attractive, and (8) humorous. Place the tags on appropriate objects or near an event that is occurring in a defined area. You must use the tags that best describe what *you* value in the environment; however, other students may describe the same object or event by using the same or different values words.

2. After you have placed your set of tags out in an area, your instructor will make a tour to examine what each values word describes. You must be prepared to explain your choice of words. What conclusions can be drawn about how people value their surroundings from doing this?

3. Add to your list of "values" words, and repeat this activity, using the new words.

Reflecting on the Experience:

1. Which "values" words were used the most by the group? . . . used the least?

2. Which objects were viewed with similar "values" words? . . . with dissimilar "values" words?

3. What new "values" words would you add to more tags the next time you do this activity?

Dam Decisions:

Find an area outside which could possible be flooded by the construction of a dam, and imagine that the area will be flooded and destroyed because of the building of a dam. Rank the three most valuable resources to be saved by moving them before the area is flooded. Support your first and last choices with reasons. Attempt to reach a group consensus about what to save first. (A group consensus is a decision in which all members of your group could "live with" the choice, even though it may not be first on their list.)

Reflecting on the Experience:

1. Could your group reach a consensus in a reasonable length of time?

2. Did some students change their ordering of what to save because of reasons given by others?

3. Would some students change their ordering if told that a living resource would not survive a move?

4. Did it matter if the resource was animate (alive) or inanimate (not living)?

5. Were some objects not considered as natural resources? If so, which ones? Why?

6. Can some natural resources become a pest or a problem? If so, which ones?

When Does Sound Become Noise?:

1. When sound is judged to be disagreeable, it becomes noise. Noise is a values judgment—the same sound can be called a noise by some people and a pleasant sound by others. Think about how different people describe music.

2. Go outdoors, and listen for sounds around you. To gather more sound, enlarge your outer ears by cupping them with your hands. On a piece of paper, draw a horizontal line. At one end place the word "noise" and at the other end place the words, "pleasant sound." As you hear a sound, place the name of the source on the line in the "correct" location according to how you feel about the sound.

3. If you cannot identify the source, place a sound symbol on the line so that you can remember it. Sound symbols are lines that show sound visually. For example:

| Ringing | Ambulance | Cuckoo |
| alarm clock | siren | clock |

4. Once several sounds have been heard and the appropriate words or symbols placed on the line in the proper place, decide as a group which are pleasant sounds and which are noise. Can you reach a consensus?

Reflecting on the Experience:

1. Are all sounds of nature pleasant?

2. Are all sounds made by persons or what they manufacture unpleasant?

3. Can you explain why you decided what you did?

4. What problems arise when people disagree about noise?

5. How can we solve problems created by different ways of valuing sounds?

Declaration of Dependence:

1. While sitting comfortably outdoors, memorize, recite, or read aloud the *Declaration of Dependence* by Henry Gibson.

2. As each line is spoken, try to imagine what Mr. Gibson might have been feeling and visualizing in his mind.

I am part of Nature
I am part of everything that lives
I am bound together with all living things in air, in land, in water.
My life depends upon Nature—
Upon its balance, upon its resources, and upon the continuity of both.
To destroy them is to destroy myself.
As a member of the human race
I am responsible for its survival.
I am part of Nature.
I will not destroy it.

3. Find examples of how you are "a part of everything that lives" in the air, on land, and in the water.

4. What can you see that you consider to be "Nature"? What is not a part of "Nature"?

5. Find examples of how your life depends upon Nature's "balance" and upon its "resources."

6. Find examples of how destroying part of Nature is "to destroy" yourself.

7. Write your own version of *Declaration of Dependence,* and think of a different title for it.

Reflecting on the Experience:

1. Does the word "nature" have different meanings to different people? What are some of them?

2. If we really believed that we are part of nature, would we behave differently? How?

3. Without nature what would our lives be like?

Picky, Picky!

Deciding whether or not to pick plants for some use can be a difficult values decision. For example, some people believe that flowers should never be picked because their beauty lasts longer growing on the plant. Others pick flowers and other plant parts for bouquets or table centerpieces, while still others pick only certain kinds of flowers. How can you decide? Deciding what to pick and what not to pick involves becoming clear about your values regarding plants. Before picking a plant, ask yourself the following questions:

1. Is the plant protected by law?

2. Is it rare in the area?

3. Do animals benefit from it?

4. Is it a health or safety hazard?

5. Can you make something more useful or beautiful from it?

6. Can you learn something more about it by picking it?

7. Will the area be improved by its removal?

8. Will the plant die soon anyway if I leave it?

9. Will I be harmed by the plant if I pick it?

10. Is it right to destroy a living thing without a good reason?

After answering each question, how can you decide whether or not to pick a plant? You must decide what you value most, and then act accordingly.

Go outside and select a plant. Carefully consider each question before deciding whether or not to pick it.

Reflecting on the Experience:

1. Are there some plants that should never be picked?

2. Are there some plants that can always be picked?

3. What values were important to you before deciding to pick a plant?

4. Could we survive if we didn't destroy some plants?

5. Can you make a list of rules about picking plants in your area?

When Is a Plant a Weed?

A weed is a plant out of place. There-fore, a rose could be considered a weed if it grew in an onion patch. Whether or not a plant is called a weed depends upon a person's values. Some people call dandelions weeds when they grow in lawns where they are not wanted. Others like to see the beautiful yellow flowers growing in the lawn and don't consider them weeds. Sometimes a dandelion is considered a weed when it grows in a lawn and a useful plant when it grows by the roadside.

Take a survey in your community to find out which plants are considered to be weeds. If you find disagreement, you will know that people's values are different concerning some plants. Does your community have any laws concerning weeds? Sometimes plants that are considered weeds can be useful for different purposes. The following plants are sometimes considered to be weeds:

Possible Weeds	Use
Dandelion	Dried roots can be a coffee substitute; young leaves can be used in salads.
Thistle	Some birds line their nests with the fluff from the seeds.
Poison Ivy	Birds eat the white berries.
Purple Loosestrife	The flowers are a beautiful purple color.
Plantain	Birds eat the seeds, and a salad can be made from young tender leaves.

Continue this chart with the information you gather from the weed survey and from reading reference books. A good reference is *Weeds,* a Golden Nature Guide.

Reflecting on the Experience:

1. Should a plant that is judged useful to animals still be called a weed?

2. Some people believe that there is no such thing as a weed and that all plants have some uses and therefore have a right to grow. Do you agree with this position?

Code of Ethics

According to Aldo Leopold, an ethic is "a limitation on freedom of action in the struggle for existence." If we are to enjoy the dwindling amount of open spaces, we need to limit the way we use these areas.

Read "The Trail User's Code of Ethics" (taken from *Environmental Education News for School People,* Michigan Department of Natural Resources) as you take a walk along a trail in a woods or field. Find and discuss examples of how each item in the code applies at certain locations along the trail. Look for evidence that previous users did *not* follow some of the items of the Code.

The Trail User's Code of Ethics

1. I will appreciate the solitude and beauty of the trail and the surrounding environment. I will respect the feelings of others toward it.

2. I will do my best to preserve the natural and historic features which attracted me to the trail.

3. I will not disturb plant and animal wildlife along the trail.

4. I will use only established campsites and rest areas when available.

5. I will reduce the litter problem by carrying out all that I take in and more.

6. I will take care to conserve the improvements that have been placed along the trail.

7. I will use a trail only for its designated purpose.

8. I will not promote activities or create situations that disturb others.

9. I will promote the use of maps, educational materials and equipment that will help trail users achieve maximum enjoyment.

10. I will exercise utmost care with open fires.

11. I will not exceed my physical or technical capabilities and will travel equipped to meet emergency situations.

12. I will treat property of others with the same care I would give my own property by not entering posted land, by observing laws and regulations and by discouraging violations of them, by getting permission before entering private property, and by not disturbing livestock nor passing over cultivated fields.

After your walk, write your own code of ethics for using a natural area, local park, or school grounds. What items were added to your list of environmental values in the code?

Reflecting on the Experience:

1. When you compare the codes of ethics written by different people, can you detect various values expressed?

2. Do you think it would ever be possible to write a code of ethics that everyone in your class could agree to follow? . . . in your school? . . . in your community?

A Teacher's Environmental Code of Ethics

I will teach only that which is life affirming:
the preservation, reclamation, and protection of our planet home.

I will teach connections:
the myriad of ways that plants, soil, rocks, trees, animals, and humans
are dependent on and enriched by one another.

I will teach respect for the rights of all others to a peaceful and
natural existence:
plants, animals, people; regardless of national affiliation, political
persuasion, economic condition, race, religion, or gender.

I will teach peace:
with other people, with the flora and fauna, with the entire biotic
organism.

I will teach tolerance of other views:
knowing that there are many approaches to even the tallest mountain,
but always the universal goal.

I will teach giving back:
time, energy, matter; by recycling, working for environmental groups
and causes, using biodegradable materials, planting trees, growing prairies.

I will teach appreciation for wonder and beauty of our planet home:
the shape of a cloud scudding across a summer sky, the autumn beauty
of a phalanx of geese responding to an ancient call, the quiet solitude
of a snowy wood at twilight, the joyful and raucous riot of color that
is a spring meadow.

I will teach the joy to be found outdoors:

I will take my students out of doors:

I will let the outdoors teach them . . . and me.

Maureen Zarrella
Proviso Area Exceptional Children's Center
Maywood, IL

XVIII. Initiative Tasks

"Initiative Tasks," or "Initiative Activities," are often used to challenge groups of students by requiring them to draw upon their "inner resources." These are problem-oriented activities in which it is necessary for the members of the group to work together in order to reach a solution. In doing so, the students suggest possible approaches; discuss their solutions; attempt to try them out; and regroup, evaluate, and test new approaches until they succeed.

To be an "initiative task" the problem must (1) be challenging to the group; (2) require the involvement of all members; and (3) involve risk, confusion, pain, discomfort, and failure, as well as success.

Staff training is the most important aspect of developing an initiatives program, and in most instances, it is necessary that this be provided at the onset. In some instances, it may become necessary to employ individuals who are interested in, and who have the skills needed for, the particular adventure/initiative activity.

Leaders of initiatives programs must have the physical skills and competencies necessary for the tasks involved. They must master teaching techniques conducive to group involvement and cohesion. Sympathetic leaders, who understand group interpersonal relationships, can also bring about much more enjoyable and educational experiences for those involved than can those leaders who lack such skills.

Leaders must also be skilled in the art of evaluating, or processing. An immediate evaluation of an attempted solution of an activity brings the attention of the participants to themselves as individuals as well as members of the group. Having participants discuss the actions that were successful, and those that were not, and the reasons for the successes or failures, should be accomplished without "putting anyone down." Good leaders should work to instill a sense of "group" awareness in all participants and acknowledge each and every participant's contributions to all activities.

Preparation for Initiatives

The leader sets the stage and informs the group of the objectives, or reasons, for being involved in the problem and explains the rules. Once the general information about the task and the limitations, or parameters, have been given, the group moves toward a solution.

Leaders must address the following questions when planning for initiatives:

1.   What expectations are reasonable and achievable for the particular group?

2.   What resources, sites or locations, and equipment or materials are needed to begin the program?

3.   What new skills are needed, and how are they to be obtained?

4.   What are the appropriate activities?

5.   What rules and guidelines must be established for the activity? (This includes warnings about potential hazards.)

6.   What procession is needed to provide reinforcement and follow-up for the participants?

7.   What evaluative criteria are needed to provide a basis for discussion and change in the program in the future?

Because initiative tasks may involve a variety of activities, obstacles or challenges, and environments, a checklist such as presented here may help to insure a program that is safe and well adapted to the needs of the group. This checklist is divided into three phases: (1) pre-activity, (2) actual participation, and (3) post-activity.

Pre-activity:

1.   Make a visual check of the area, all equipment, connections, and materials.

2.   Remove any deadfall, branches, or other objects which may cause injury to participants.

3.   Check all knots, cables, ropes, ladders, clips, bolts, lashings, and first-aid equipment.

Actual Participation:

1.   Orient the group to the site, the task to be encountered, the objectives of the activity, and the reasons for doing the activity, and make known your expectations of the group.

2. Lead the group through a step-by-step "walk-through" for each task, or activity, giving information about each but not offering solutions.

3. Give clear and concise directions for spotting, and explain the need for spotting.

4. Give specific instructions for the first activity, and provide demonstrations. Deal with the objective, or goal, and the rules for completing the activity.

5. Evaluate and discuss each phase of the activity as needed, and present a "wrap-up" summary covering the entire session.

Post-activity:

1. Collect, count, clean, and store equipment.

2. Report information about the status of the equipment, site, materials, etc., and compile a permanent record.

3. Report any injuries and "near misses" that happened to any of the participants, and explain the details of each occurrence. In retrospect, offer a solution as to how each one could have been prevented.

Administrators should keep in contact with all facets of the initiatives program and become involved in decisions about staff training, the specific activities to be used, structures to be built, and modifications made in the program.

Introductory Initiatives

Begin with the following activities when starting a program of initiatives. Follow them with more difficult tasks once the unit of the group develops.

Individual Trust Fall. Members of the group should pair up so that one of the pair acts as the "catcher" and the other as the "faller." The catcher stands erect behind the faller, who stands stiff with arms at sides. (The catcher must be made aware of the need to catch the faller and to especially protect the head.)

Upon the command "falling" the catcher responds with "fall on" if ready. The faller then falls backward to be caught by the catcher's arms. After a bit, the catcher moves slightly backward from the faller, and the process is repeated. The catcher is not permitted to move away more than one-half the height of the person falling. After the skills of catching and falling have been developed, the two should change positions and repeat. A safer falling posture is for the faller to outstretch the arms to prevent any chance of falling through the arms of the catcher.

Group Ring Trust. Eight to 12 participants form a tight circle facing inward, with one member, the "faller," inside the circle. The faller stands stiff with hands to the side and falls outward to be caught and pushed back into an upright position. The faller continues to fall in different directions as members catch and then push the faller upright. Each person takes a turn at being the faller.

Backward Trust Fall. At least seven "catchers" (preferably nine) align themselves in two parallel rows about one-half arm's length apart and with one person at the head end of each of the rows. This provides an alignment in the form of a "U" with the open end toward a stump, wall, or ladder where the "faller" will be.

The catchers nearest the wall or ladder assist the faller to climb to the proper height, about 1.25 meters (4 feet). The faller aligns the two rows with the head catcher to insure adequate room for the fall. When the faller is ready and satisfied with the alignment of the catchers, the command of "falling" is given, and the catchers as a group respond, if ready, with "fall on." Then the faller stiffens, places arms across the waist, and falls backward to be caught by the group of catchers. Each group member takes a turn at being "faller." Should the faller "butt fudge" or bend at the waist, he or she must climb back and refall.

When group members are aligned in the rows for catching, they must have their arms outstretched with palms up, with an arm from one catcher alternating with that of the catcher from the opposite row. The "head" catchers should have hands outstretched, with palms up and slightly higher than those of the "end" catchers in order to handle the faller's head and protect it from injury. The catchers are not allowed to lock arms or wrists. There is greater chance of injury to both the catchers and the fallers when arms are locked, as compared to the shock absorber motion of the free arm.

Group Challenges and Initiatives

No attempt has been made to classify the following initiatives as to age level or degree of difficulty, and no solutions have been suggested. There is no prescribed sequence for using these tasks. That is left to the judgment of the leader taking into consideration the unity of the group, physical capabilities of the students, and constraints of time involved.

All Aboard the Stump. A tree stump that is solid on the surface and about 30 centimeters (12 to 13 inches) in diameter is needed. A platform made especially for this activity works well. The objective is to have the entire group off the ground and onto the stump at the same time and to remain there while counting to 30. No additional equipment may be used, and no part of anyone's body may be touching the ground. The stump, or platform, should be less than 60 centimeters (2 feet) in height.

Blindfold People-Height Lineup. The group is brought to a wall, and each person is given a blindfold. At the signal from the leader, the blindfolds are put into place. The leader then directs the group to align itself along the wall from tallest to shortest. No talking, or verbal communication, is permitted.

People Pass. Participants sit on the ground between the legs of the person behind them, thus forming a long line, or chain. Everyone sits as close together as possible. One member stands at the front of the line facing the group, stretches arms out in front, and falls forward. The chain members place their hands overhead, lift the person up and pass him or her toward the rear as the person lies in a horizontal position. Upon reaching the rear of the chain, the person being passed sits down, and the individual at the head of the line becomes the body to be passed. This continues until all group members get their turn at being passed.

The Bear Paw. Folks in the north woods country say that you can tell how high a bear will climb by the claw marks on the tree. This group task is to make a mark as high on a designated tree, or pole, as possible by using only the group members themselves. The mark may be made by using chalk or by tying colored twine around the tree. No climbing of the tree is permitted.

Piggin String. The group is formed into a very compact circle facing outward. A long rope, the piggin string, is wrapped around them in a tight loop. The group then walks a given distance and direction. The distance traversed should contain different inclines and directions so that all group members get to move forward as well as backward.

Centipede Walk. This is a "centipede" version of the three-legged walk. This require two boards, 4 centimeters by 8 centimeters by 3 meters (2 inches by 4 inches by 10 feet), with holes drilled at about 30-centimeter (1-foot) intervals through the thickness dimension. A 1-meter (3-foot) length of rope, knotted at one end, is fed through each hole so that all long ends are at the top sides of the boards. The two boards are placed parallel on the ground about 30 centimeters (1 foot) apart. Each player places one foot on each board, picks up a rope from each board for handles, and waits for a signal to walk over a straight course for a pre-designated distance. In unison, the players lift their feet and the boards simultaneously, left, right, left, right, etc. If any of the players fall off or touch the ground with their foot, the entire group returns to the starting place and attempts it again.

The Electric Fence. Two uprights, 3 meters (10 feet) apart have two ropes placed horizontally between them, the lower one about crotch height. The top one should be about chest high. (Use the average height for the particular group.) A shallow, round cake pan is filled with ACID (water). The challenge is for the group members (five or six) to place at least one hand on the pan, jointly lift the ACID, and carry it through the "electrified fence" without being electrocuted or having any ACID spill. If any ACID spills, any hand leaves the pan, or if an individual touches the "fence," the group starts over.

NOTE: The usual "electric fence" configuration that has a high wire or rope that the group must go over using a pole for assistance is not recommended because of the injury potential of the height that the group members must traverse.

The Tunnel. A large culvert or drain tile about 100 centimeters (3½ feet) in diameter is used as the tunnel. Half of the group begins from one end of the tunnel and the other half from the other end. One by one they crawl through the tunnel, passing the rest of the people coming from the opposite direction.

A variation is to have two small wood blocks for hand rests and a 1-meter (3-foot) long piece of a 2 × 4 for a foot piece. Members crawl through the tunnel using only these three insulators. Should they touch any part of the tunnel with their body, they must being again. When a member gets to the opposite end, the three wood pieces are thrown back through the tunnel to the other group members.

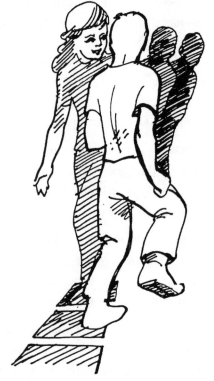

Traffic Jam. Squares of plywood, cardboard, or similar material, about 30 centimeters (1 foot) on a side, are laid out in a straight line. There should be one more square than participants. The group is divided into two parts and aligned on the squares, starting at each outside end and progressing toward the middle, leaving a "free" square between each segment of the group.

Upon command, the group members move forward and attempt to position themselves on squares on the opposite side of the "free" square. No more than one person may be on a square at a time, but a member may step around another person if there is a blank square available on the other side.

The objective of this initiative is for the members to pass through the free area and realign themselves on the opposite side of the free square. A variation of this activity is to draw squares with chalk on a blacktop surface.

If logs can be found in a wooded area, they can be arranged to form a large circle. Two groups, each consisting of the same number of players, should line up in the circle, facing each other. A starting point should be designated for each group. At a signal, the players start walking on the logs toward each other. The object is to pass around the members of the opposite group as they traverse the circle of logs. If anyone falls off of a log, that player must return to the starting point and begin again. The group that returns to the starting place first is the winner; provided, of course, that all players of that group finally made it around the circle without falling off.

More Initiatives and Challenges

Search and Rescue. The group moves to a large open area where there is little chance of injury due to vegetation or terrain differences. The players are shown the outer limits of the area in which they will be working, and then all but one of the players are blindfolded. The task is to find the lost group member, who moves about with no noise and attempts to avoid the touch of fellow members, who also move about with no verbal communication.

A variation is the *Antelope and the Wolf,* or the *Predator and Prey,* in which, in most instances, the hunter makes the noise of an animal (wolf or other predator), and the prey makes another noise (antelope or other prey)—but all prey are blindfolded.

Tent Erection. Players are divided into groups of about four. Each group is given the challenge of erecting the tent while blindfolded. A good self-contained tent with poles must be provided. This activity may be done inside, as well as outside, if enough additional people are available to act as "tent stakes."

Many tent manufacturers claim that their tents may be erected in 3 to 5 minutes, but give this blindfolded group at least 10 minutes. Repeat until all members of the original group have had a chance to perform as a tent erection team. It is better if all members can be active at the same time so that they can compare results.

The Stretcher Case. A group member is "injured" so that the group must come up with an emergency litter, or stretcher. The group is in a ravine or below a wall that requires the litter to be lifted above the wall and then carried the given distance. Two poles, each about 2½ meters (8 feet) long are made available, but the group must come up with its own solution of developing a litter and lifting and carrying it out of the area. No materials other than the two poles will be available as extra materials.

The Maze. The group members are blindfolded and led by the leader to a specific area, where a maze of string or small rope has been set up. Players line up, and place their left hand on the shoulder of the person ahead of them, keeping that position throughout the game. The leader positions the first player by the line and instructs him or her to grasp the line with his or her right hand. The players use their right hand to find and hold onto the line and follow the line to the end. The maze should zigzag and cover a variety of inclines and terrains. When they reach the end of the line, the players remove their blindfolds and attempt to retrace their steps.

Monster. The participants are divided into two groups and instructed to form a "monster" by attaching themselves to each other by joining hands or by linking arms or legs, being very careful to have only one hand or one foot on the ground at a time. They should develop a specific animal sound and make that sound as they move a specified distance. Any time anyone has more than one foot or hand on the ground, the entire group has to return to the starting point and begin again. The group that successfully travels the required distance first is the winner.

A variation is the *Machine,* in which the sound that is developed is the sound of some type of machine, rather than an animal sound. Each player does a specific motion of a machine as the "machine" moves the required distance.

Lap Sit. Each member of the group stands in a tight circle, shoulder to shoulder. Then the players turn to the right upon command and very gently sit down on the lap of the person behind them. If and when the procedure is successfully completed, the circle will attempt to "walk" in unison in the seated position, either clockwise (backward) or counterclockwise (forward) as directed, making at least one complete circle.

Advanced Initiatives Requiring Structures

In most cases, permanent structures are required for the following activities. Educational organizations are establishing more and more initiatives courses which contain the structures needed to safely complete challenges like these. Those who are considering the development of initiatives courses should work with competent consultants to assure that their structures are constructed properly and that their program and procedures are safe.

Beam. A log, about 15 centimeters (6 inches) in diameter, is appropriate for the "beam" used in this activity. It must be securely fixed at a height suitable for the group involved. (The tallest player should be able to reach the top of the beam with an outstretched arm.) Courses erected permanently often have the beam at a height of about 2 meters (6 feet).

The objective is to get all of the players over the top of the beam as quickly as possible. No more than three members of the team are allowed up on the beam at a time, and after one has crossed the beam, that person may only act as a "spotter" to help break any falls.

Team members on the starting side (waiting their turn to cross the beam) should act as "spotters," "pushers," and "lifters" to assist their team members to get over the top.

CAUTION: Always have sufficient spotters, alert and ready for any fall.

Wall. The "wall" is similar to the "beam" but more difficult. The wall is of solid construction, usually 3 to 3½ meters (10 to 11 feet) high, with a platform on the backside for participants to stand on. The objective is to take all members of the group over the top of the wall in as short a time as possible. No more than three players should be allowed on the platform at a time. Once a player has been raised over the wall and returned to ground level, that person should act as a spotter, but may *not,* however, assist in the lifting of other team members. Players must not use the edges or ends of the wall or any device or material that the leader rules as inappropriate. Again, all available team members must act as spotters to help prevent any falls or injuries. The last player has to jump high enough to catch the hand of one of the players on the platform.

Nitro Crossing. This is a modification of the old *Tarzan Swing,* which calls for all members of the group to traverse a "chasm" that may either be deep or be filled with human-eating animals or chemicals. The objective is to get across the space in a minimal time, using only the Tarzan vertical rope as an assist. The challenge also calls for carrying across an open container of NITRO (water) without spilling it.

If any of the members touch ground between the entrance and exit areas, they must return and attempt to cross again. If any NITRO is spilled, all members must return and begin again.

Equipment consists of a 2½-centimeter (1-inch) rope hanging from a large tree or structure to about ½ meter (18 inches) above the ground. A monkey-fist, or overhand knot, is tied on the loose end of the rope. Start and stop lines are drawn about 5 meters (15 feet) on either side of the freely hanging rope. No other material may be used by the group. Stepping over the start and stop lines is prohibited and requires returning to start anew.

Caber Toss. A "caber" is a pole approximately 2½ meters (8 feet) in length and about 10 centimeters (4 inches) in diameter. The objective is for each member of the group to toss the caber as far as possible.

The pole should be held in a horizontal position with the "tosser's" hands interlocked below the pole. Upon the given signal, the caber is lifted and thrown forward as far as possible with one effort. The distance is measured for each team member, and a total distance score is obtained for the group.

Log Walk. Several logs about 15 centimeters (6 inches) in diameter are fixed horizontally 1 meter (3 feet) or more above the ground. It is more challenging if some are inclined slightly so that each succeeding log is slightly higher than the previous one.

The objective is for each member of the group to walk the logs without falling. Other members of the group act as spotters for the walker. Only one walker is allowed at a time, and all other group members should be alert, functioning as spotters along the entire length of the logs.

Tire Removal. An upright pole of about 3½ meters (11 feet) in length is needed for this challenge. A tire is placed over the pole. The task for the group is to remove the tire from the pole.

The group may use no material other than what it has brought; and no one may "shinny up" or "straddle" the pole. A group effort is required to remove the tire, bring it to the ground, and then replace it. Spotters should always be used.

IMPORTANT: Many of these games and activities require the students to move about, sometimes swiftly. Teachers should always be alert to the potential hazards and student behaviors that can lead to injury. Care should be taken to assure that students are constantly supervised and that sites chosen for activities of this type are safe and free of obstacles and objects on which the students could fall or be injured.

XIX. Creating Humane Learning Climates

Meteorologists define the word "climate" as the average condition of the weather at a place over a period of years. Factors such as temperature, wind velocity, humidity, and precipitation are all taken into account. Educators define the word "climate" in a similar way, but they use it to describe the atmosphere or general tone of a learning experience. They consider human factors such as respect, trust, morale, opportunities for input, growth and renewal, cohesiveness, and caring.

A humane climate can be created in a group if the individuals practice certain personal and interpersonal skills.

Personal skills are those capacities that allow individuals to gain access to their feelings, including the ability to discriminate among a range of different emotions, to identify them accurately, and to use them in understanding and directing personal behavior. Interpersonal skills are those capacities that allow individuals to notice and respond to others by making distinctions among their temperaments, motivations, and intentions. They enable individuals to understand and sometimes to influence group dynamics.

Nature can provide us with a setting in which we can learn about ourselves and others. So often we separate nature from human nature—birds or trees from people. Nature can be used as a mirror for us to better understand human behavior. Outdoor teachers should consider their students as part of the environment to be observed and treated as carefully as a tiny flower along the trail.

Using the outdoors as a place to reflect upon thoughts and feelings about people is not a new idea. For centuries Orientals have used art and literature to express their interconnectedness with nature. To many Chinese and Japanese, all living and non-living things—mountains, flowers, children, and water—are part of a universal creation. Nature is so important to the people of the Orient that even when poets write about their personal feelings, they often mention things like the summer winds or a singing bird.

Before we can plan to use the outdoors to improve personal and interpersonal skills, we must see the interconnections among nature and human nature. Virginia Eifert saw a connection between herself and the earth when she wrote:

> I stand by the river and know that it has been here yesterday and will be here tomorrow and that therefore, since I am part of its pattern today, I also belong to all its yesterdays and will be part of all its tomorrows. This is a kind of earthly immortality, a kinship with rivers and hills and rocks, with all things and all creatures that have ever lived or ever will live or have their being on the earth.

> Written on a plaque in the Illinois State Museum, Springfield, Illinois.

The following outdoor activities have been used successfully by teachers and other youth leaders to bring about greater awareness of personal and interpersonal skills.

The What, Why, and How of Community Building

What?:

Community building is a process and a goal that some groups undergo and achieve. It involves a gradual change of stages, beginning with a collection of individuals and progressing to a close-knit group characterized by feelings of oneness and identity. Community members share a set of core values and knowledge while, at the same time, respect the diversity within the group. Communities function with a set of agreed upon norms or standards of behavior which enable the members to cooperate, trust, communicate, and care about each other. Community members recognize that everyone wants to feel included. They have the potential to expand their feelings of unity, regress to former stages, or split up completely.

Why?:

Community building skills are important to learn and practice because:

1. People have a basic need to belong to social groups.

2. People working together are better able to solve problems and make wise decisions which result in change and improvement of their environment.

3. Most people can learn and retain concepts and information better in groups than as individuals.

4. Democratic societies are organized more on the basis of cooperation than on competition.

5. Groups are the best context in which to master personal and interpersonal skills.

How?:

The building blocks of a community are many and varied. The most important foundation is a desire by all to build and maintain the community structure. The building blocks consist of personal attitudes and interpersonal skills. Here are some of the most important ones:

—I believe in the value of people and their abilities to resolve conflicts constructively.

—I want to be recognized and praised for my inner goodness and accomplishments if your praise is genuine.

—I need you and others and value your support and encouragement.

—Your trust for me can grow when I earn it through my positive interactions with you.

—When I am open and truthful with you about who I really am, you will grow to respect me more.

—It is worthwhile to limit some of my freedoms for the good of the whole community.

—I can disagree with your opinions, but still accept you as a valuable person.

—If I attempt to see the world from your perspective and listen to you attentively, I may understand you better.

—Having a clear purpose for our community and knowing how to reach our goals, helps me feel more effective and in control of my life.

—Knowing and accepting the rules and norms for operating in a community helps to reduce conflicts.

Personal Skills and Outdoor Activities

This section lists some personal skill objectives followed by an outdoor activity to use in practicing each one.

Objective: To become aware of personal feelings.

Activity: Another Kind of Laundry List

Procedure: Instruct the students to:

Go outside and sit alone for 15 minutes. On a piece of paper make two columns. Label one "Feelings," the other "Thoughts." Under the correct heading, write the thoughts and feelings you experience while sitting.

Reflecting on
the Experience: Which list was longer? Which list was more difficult to make? Check the words in each column to make sure they are in the correct place. Was it difficult to distinguish a thought from a feeling?

When I hide my emotions, my stomach keeps score.

Anonymous

Objective: To be able to affirm personal worth.

Activity: Nature Mirrors

Procedure: Instruct the students to:

Locate the following things and then share with a partner the ways that your personal strengths are like these objects:

1.	Tree	5.	Water
2.	Rock	6.	Cloud
3.	Seed	7.	Pavement
4.	Sun	8.	Soil

Expand the list and find more ways in which you are like these objects.

Reflecting on
the Experience: How did it feel to share your personal strengths with someone? Which object did you like best? Why? How can you continue to affirm yourself in the future?

> If you can do it, it ain't brag.
>
> Dizzy Dean

Objective: To demonstrate a sense of humor.

Activity: Natural Humor Handles

Procedure: Instruct the students to:

Go outside and find natural objects to use as humor handles. For example, an acorn cap can be described as an oak sprout beanie or as a small bowl for hot "oakmeal." Select at least three objects, and return to the group to share your "natural highs."

Reflecting on
the Experience: Does this type of humor search help you to see the people around you in new ways, too? Ask the people in your group who show a good sense of humor how they went about coming up with such funny lines. Do you think that you can create some guidelines for being funny?

> Humor is like love; the more you give away
>   The more you end up receiving.
>
> Joel Goodman

Objective: To recognize personal power.

Activity: Natural Power

Procedure: Instruct the students to:

Go outside and find examples of powerful natural objects and events. Complete the following sentences by filling in the blanks for each example you find. "The _____ is powerful because _____." After completing at least five sentences, substitute the words "I am" for the object or event and experience how it feels to say each sentence. For example: "The stream is powerful because it slowly wears away rocks." "I am powerful because I slowly wear away rocks."

Reflecting on the Experience:	Does the metaphor fit something you feel powerful doing? Would it help to change the sentence slightly to fit your life more closely?

> Whatever you can do, or dream you can do, begin it.
> Boldness has Genius, Power, and Magic in it.
>
> Goethe

Objective:	To take appropriate risks.
Activity:	Dumbo's® Feather
Procedure:	Dumbo®, the big-eared Disney cartoon elephant, thought that he could fly because of a magic feather he held in his trunk. When he accidentally dropped the feather while at the top of a circus ladder, he discovered that he could fly without it. The feather had helped him take a risk and to believe in himself.

Instruct the students to:

Find an object outside that will help you take a risk by doing something to make your life better. After you have found the object, show it to the group and tell what you would like to be better able to do.

Reflecting on the Experience:	Can you think of other objects that people believe can help them perform better? How do you gain confidence in risk taking when you want to change something in your life?

> We must dare, and dare again, and go on daring.
>
> George Jacques Danton

Interpersonal Skills and Outdoor Activities

This section lists some interpersonal skill objectives followed by an outdoor activity to use in practicing each one.

Objective: To communicate thoughts and feelings.

Activity: Sticks, Stones, and Two Leaves

Procedure: Instruct the students to:

Choose a partner and gather matching sets of two sticks (each a different size), four rocks (each a different size), and two leaves (preferably fallen from tree). They should be matched as closely as possible for length, width, thickness, etc. Sit back-to-back in a comfortable place with the set of eight objects on the ground in front of each of you. One of you be the follower and one the leader. The leader arranges the eight items in a pattern on the ground and then attempts to describe the arrangement to the follower. The follower must make the same arrangement as the leader but cannot speak or look around throughout the exercise. When the follower completes the task, check to see how accurately it was done. Switch roles and repeat the activity. Discuss how the task would have been different if the follower had been allowed to ask questions. If time permits, repeat the activity allowing the follower to talk. Discuss the difference that verbal feedback makes in communicating clearly.

Reflecting on
the Experience: Was the task easier to do after analyzing the problems encountered during the first time around? How would asking questions of the leader help the follower do a better job?

> There is nothing so wonderful as a good idea;
> there is nothing so tragic as a good idea
> which cannot be communicated.
>
> Ely

Objective: To empathize with others.

Activity: Empathy Peeking

Procedure: Instruct the students to:

Sit face-to-face with your partner in a comfortable place outside. Ask your partner to take three minutes to mention everything that comes into his or her awareness. After your partner finishes, share some thoughts and feelings that occurred to you while you were sharing your partner's awareness experiences. Repeat the exercise, and this time share your awarenesses with your partner. Ask for feedback when you finish your three-minute session.

Reflecting on
the Experience: Are you better able to empathize with your partner now? Did your partner help you become aware of new things in your surroundings? How did knowing more about your partner's awareness help you to know and appreciate your partner better?

> It is not often that I meet someone with whom I can feel
> a deep oneness, a feeling that we have met before, that
> we have shared the same experiences and thoughts
> some place else a long time ago.
>
> Joyce Shardin

Objective: To interpret non-verbal language.

Activity: Wildlife Watch

Procedure: Instruct the students to:

Locate an animal and carefully observe its movements. You will need to sit as motionless as possible, and you may benefit from a pair of binoculars. Make a list of the body movements that are repeated more than three times during 10 minutes of observation. Return to a central area and imitate one of the animal's characteristic movements. Make a guess about what the movement communicates. If you are in an area with a lot of people, spend 10 minutes observing their body movements.

Reflecting on
the Experience: Is it easier to make guesses about what people are communicating? If possible, ask some of the people you observed for feedback about what their body movements were intended to communicate.

> We all, in one way or another, send our little messages
> out to the world . . . and rarely do we
> send out messages consciously.
>
> Julius Fast

Objective: To be able to draw out others through questioning.

Activity: Leading Questions

Procedure: Sometimes you can lead people to new learnings by asking good questions.

Instruct the students to:

Find a place outside and write 10 questions that will help others learn something about that place. When you are finished, find a partner and ask your questions to see if that individual can learn from them. Evaluate your questions by how much the other person became aware of and learned. How many of your questions were open and how many were closed? Practice both kinds of questions by asking your partner several of each type in order to learn more about that person's life. Remember that each of you has the right to "pass" and not answer any question that seems too personal.

Reflecting on
the Experience: What kinds of questions resulted in the most information about the place or the person? What type of questions did you feel most comfortable answering? Least comfortable?

A wise question is half of knowledge.

Lord Bacon

Objective: To be able to validate others.

Activity: Food Chain Validating

Procedure: Instruct the students to:

Individually or in small groups, locate evidence of a natural food chain. On paper, fill in as many links of the chain as possible, even if you cannot see immediate evidence of each link. Image that each living or non-living thing in the chain could speak. How would each validate (verbally appreciate the value of someone) another in the food chain?

For example, in the familiar food chain of owl, snake, frog, insect, plant, sun, the owl might say to the snake, "You are skillful in hiding in the grass." The snake might say to the frog, "You are a better underwater swimmer than I am." The frog might say to the insect, "You can fly very fast to escape my sticky tongue." After each person or group shares food chain validations, ask the others to key in on something to validate about people there.

245

Reflecting on
the Experience: How did you feel about giving validations for the food chain links? How did it feel to receive validations from the other members? Is giving and receiving validations a norm in your group? If not, why not?

I can live for two months on a good compliment.

Mark Twain

Putting It All Together

"What does all of this mean for my teaching?" you may ask. "How can I put all of this together and make it work?" The answers are not always simple because learning and teaching about personal and interpersonal skills often involves unknowns and sometimes unpredictables.

As leaders we know that we can't always control what is going to happen when we encourage people to explore their feelings about themselves and others. One helpful guideline is to create a safe, trusting, humane climate by allowing students to go only as deeply into the activity as they wish. Always establish and enforce the ground rule that everyone has the right and privilege to "pass" or not share feelings. Another helpful guideline is to trust your judgment when selecting an activity for others. It must seem "right," and you must be able to clearly understand some valid reasons for conducting the activity. If you believe that the world will be a better place if people have more personal and interpersonal skills *and* that you can help them gain these through carefully selected and structured experiences, then you will be anxious to accept this invitation to explore nature and human nature through creating humane climates outdoors.

Helpful References

Cornell, Joseph Bharat, *Sharing Nature with Children,* Ananda Publications, Nevada City, California, 1979.

Knapp, Clifford E., and Joel Goodman, *Humanizing Environmental Education: A Guide for Leading Nature and Human Nature Activities,* American Camping Association, Martinsville, Indiana, 1981. (out-of-print)

Knapp, Clifford E., *Creating Humane Climates Outdoors: A People Skills Primer,* ERIC Clearing House on Rural Education and Small Schools, Charleston, West Virginia, 1988.

Van Matre, Steve, *Sunship Earth: An Acclimatization Program for Outdoor Learning,* American Camping Association, Martinsville, Indiana, 1979.

XX. Not Just an Extended Field Trip: Resident Outdoor Education (ROE)

In its simplest terms resident outdoor education (ROE) takes place when teachers and children leave their usual school setting for another site or location to remain for several days and nights. At this new location, instruction directly related to the school program is provided throughout the day and into the evening. This somewhat clinical description fails to capture the true essence of the residential experience. Perhaps this is because it is difficult to put into words the value of an experience that is often remembered by students as the highlight of their educational careers, or to describe why parents, twenty years later, take their children to visit the place where, when they were children, they spent three magical days learning about the environment.

Programs like this have been looked upon as the capstone—the apex of outdoor education. For schools where an emphasis is placed on making the most effective use of all available resources in the curriculum, the resident outdoor education experience provides a logical extension to the creative and productive use of learning environments. ROE provides the same positive outcomes and opportunities as expected in any outdoor education program. Building on children's natural curiosity and enthusiasm for learning, ROE involves first-hand, direct experiences with the environment. Concepts are learned through observed reality rather than through more abstract methods. Additionally, the residential setting provides an expanded time frame and the ability to focus curricular attention on the desired learnings. It is the contention of outdoor educators that the most effective application of resources is made when teachers use the school and nearby sites regularly, take field trips when appropriate, and provide one or more resident experiences for all the children as they move through the grades. Those communities in which ROE is the only use made of outdoor resources miss much of the potential of outdoor programming.

Historically, activities of this sort were referred to as "school camping" or "camping education." As time has passed, goals, objectives, approaches, and nearly everything about the experience has evolved and changed. A constant, perhaps, is that teachers and children, working and living together for such periods of time, accomplish much that is not possible in the school setting. Research suggests that this involvement can have positive impacts on students' socialization skills, cooperation, and tolerance for people from differing backgrounds. The potential of ROE has not been lost on parents, teachers, and students. Rooted in over fifty years of history, interest in ROE continues to increase. Even in times of fiscal austerity, schools have found ROE to be "one of the few nice things they can do for their children at little expense to the school."

This chapter will help teachers critically consider the option of providing an ROE experience and help those who decide to do so with their planning. Topics discussed will include:

1.   A Rationale for ROE

2.   Setting Your Goals and Objectives

3.   Organizational and Logistical Issues

4.   ROE as a Model for Learning and Living

A Rationale for ROE

As a rule, one finds the staunchest proponents of ROE among its practitioners. Believing in the concept, they try it out, get "hooked," and find sufficient reinforcement from being a participant in the experience itself. On the other hand, those who do not use such experiences may be less convinced that benefits coming from just three or four days of ROE are enough to justify the time away from the classroom and the work that goes into them.

Overall, ROE helps schools achieve their ongoing goals and objectives. Although there are no specific goals and objectives for ROE above and beyond those set forth by the school, there are a set of educational goals to which ROE experiences contribute most: (1) socialization, (2) self-concept or self-perception, (3) building on school subjects, (4) development of process skills, and (5) environmental awareness and understanding. Nevertheless, researchers find that such goals must be provided for when planning. Otherwise, goal attainment is haphazard at best.

Resident programs provide many opportunities for children and teachers to improve social skills. Sleeping with friends in dormitories (or tents), eating across the table from them, singing songs together at campfires, and sharing adventures all contribute to a sense of fellowship—especially when done under the eye of a caring and understanding teacher. Unfortunately, because of busy home schedules and changing family patterns, the resident experience may provide one of the few times that a child experiences a family-style meal where the focus is on good conversation and appropriate table manners. Resident centers often find that children do not know how to set a table or serve a meal. Important lessons for socialization can be built into each experience from the morning routine of cleaning the dormitory to enjoying the evening meal together.

Being away from home, perhaps for the first time; being responsible for one's self; and taking on new challenges and having success with them all contribute to the child's feeling of self-worth. Many ROE programs focus on this aspect and provide experiences especially valuable for self-concept development. Teachers report that students who may have enjoyed few educational successes in the traditional classroom seem to bloom during outdoor education programs. These successes, though seemingly minor, do contribute to a more positive self-image and attitude toward learning. This is an outcome, however, which researchers find *must* be provided for if it is to occur.

Traditionally, ROE programs have been helpful when it comes to achieving objectives in school subjects such as mathematics, science, social studies, and language arts. The setting may provide the perfect opportunity for the science teacher to compare ecosystems. Math teachers may apply indirect measurement techniques to learn the distance to the far shore of the river or lake, and social studies comes alive during an examination of how early pioneers relied upon natural resources in their daily lives. Furthermore, such adventures provide something real to write about in language arts classes. Campfires are a natural for the music teacher. Be careful when building on the school subjects; time at the ROE site is too precious to spend on what could be done as readily back at the school.

The hands-on, discovery approach to learning encourages the development of various skills. A water quality analysis of a local stream requires students to make observations, take measurements, gather data, and draw conclusions. Initiatives and low ropes courses promote the development of problem-solving and critical thinking skills. Group living, from setting tables to cleaning their dormitory rooms, encourages cooperation.

Developing understandings about the environment has long been the focus of many ROE programs and should remain the key outcome. Parents and children are traditionally highly supportive of this goal. Teachers and outdoor education staff rank it up with "self-concept" in importance. Experiencing a forest, a monarch butterfly larva, or a clean stream for the first time all help to sensitize students to the need to treat their surroundings with care and respect. The emphasis on environmental awareness and understandings within these programs has led some to suggest that a more accurate term for the experience might be "resident outdoor environmental education."

Results from hundreds of opinionnaire responses from parents, children, and teachers following their ROE experiences clearly indicate that the benefits to be derived from ROE are very real and worth the necessary time, effort, and expense to provide them. Children dwell on the highlights of their time spent at the ROE center. Parents report on the enthusiasm of their children for such experiences, and by a great majority, urge that they be conducted with greater frequency and for longer periods of time.

Setting Your Goals and Objectives

The most important and difficult decisions to make concern the goals and objectives of your ROE experience. The emphasis chosen and the objectives delineated should determine what the organizational pattern will be and what experiences or activities will be provided. If the emphasis is on science, the instruction will be primarily science related; if it is on self-concept, the instruction should provide a good measure of challenges, both physical and mental, some of which are individual and some of which require group cooperation and decision-making. Time and time again, when ROE staff ask for the school's goals and objectives, the answer comes in the form of a mere listing of activities (i.e., orienteering, water study, pioneer life). It is hard work to think through a coherent and meaningful set of goals, but it is well worth the time and effort. Without a well thought out set of goals, the program will seem haphazard, and its effectiveness will be diminished. The students will still have fun; they will still learn; but the synergy that makes a truly great program will be missing.

As you begin the process of defining your goals and objectives, consider the following questions:

1. What are your goals and objectives for outdoor-environmental education?

    a. Why are you bringing your students to the ROE center?

    b. What do you want them to get out of the experience?

2. What can be done at the ROE center to help meet school curriculum goals?

    a. What are the students studying at school just prior to and after their ROE experience?

    b. How can the ROE experience extend what is being taught in the classroom?

    c. Are there particular behaviors or skills that you are working on in the classroom?

3. What can best be taught at the ROE site? What can best be taught at or near the school?

    a. What can you teach at the ROE site that cannot be easily taught at the school?

    b. What does the outdoor environment have to offer your program?

Once you have settled on a set of goals and objectives for your ROE experience, your task becomes one of operationalizing them into a program. Some have found the use of themes to be a useful organizational tool. By developing a theme, the goals and objectives of the experience are more explicitly "tied together." For example, if the goal of the group was to build a program that would enhance the social studies curriculum, a theme surrounding "Frontier Life" might be selected. Activities could include investigations of Native American culture, pioneer skills, crafts and folklore. Similarly, if the goal was to investigate issues of developing an environmentally responsible lifestyle, a theme entitled "Caring for Our Environment" might be appropriate. Within this theme, students might study how nature recycles, prairie restoration, water quality, and environmental decision making through an evening simulation. Finally, a school that selects the goal of enhancing group cooperation might choose a theme involving "Conservation and Team Work: We're All in This Together." Students might participate in group team building activities, develop their communication skills through language arts, and work together on a conservation project that involves erosion control.

Whatever the goals and objectives, the primary issue remains: it must be abundantly clear to those designing the learning experience what is to be accomplished. Once this process is well on its way, writing lesson plans, developing schedules, and working on all the other pieces to the puzzle can begin.

Organizational and Logistical Issues

Each ROE program exhibits some unique features in its design or development. This section is intended to highlight the various ways in which an ROE experience can be devised and identify some of the options or decision points for the teacher creating such a program.

Facilities. One of the first considerations, after deciding upon an ROE program, is to ascertain where to go and what type of facility to use. To some extent this decision should be determined by the purposes and objectives of the experience. In all likelihood, it will depend upon what is available within a reasonable distance of the school. The range of site options, however, runs from tenting and open-fire cookery at a nearby camping area to the use of a resort with heated and air-conditioned rooms, gourmet meal service, and a highly qualified instructional staff. Most ROE programs use locations somewhere in-between, with facilities being more rustic than those of the latter, and instruction being provided by both site and school staff. A bit of sleuthing will probably reveal that there are a number of sites suitable for ROE within an hour or so of most schools. In a few instances, such facilities are owned and operated by school districts. Others are owned by park and forest districts, YMCA, the Scouts, or church organizations, and they can often be rented for ROE. A few colleges—and a few private individuals—provide such facilities. In recent years, zoos and museums in some major cities have adapted the resident experience for their facilities, allowing students to spend the night in a rainforest or next to the killer whale tank. School districts may even publish directories of ROE sites for the use of their teachers.

Length of Stay. In some European countries, ROE experiences of several weeks in duration are conducted. In the United States, most ROE programs run from three to five days. While a two-day/one-night experience might be a means for getting a foot in the door, the benefits of the four- or five-day program are so much greater that teachers must work toward a longer stay. Some ROE centers only take reservations for five-day programs, believing strongly that the longer period of time is necessary to accomplish educational goals. Experiences for younger children, such as third or fourth graders, however, should probably be limited to two nights at most. Cost and the availability of sites often determine what the length of time will be.

Staffing. Schools staff their ROE programs variously. While a ratio of one adult to 8 to 12 children is the norm, the type of adult leadership will depend greatly on the resources available. Some use only teachers—stripping the school of all those who can be spared for the week. Others use a minimum of teachers and depend upon parents and high school students for help with supervision. Staffing decisions are often dependent upon how much help is provided at the facility and the availability of sleeping space.

Decisions about staff must go beyond considerations of what constitutes adequate supervision. For most ROE centers, the school is expected to take at least partial responsibility for instruction. Consequently, it is important to bring sufficient numbers of chaperons to both teach and supervise the children. As you plan your staffing needs, recognize that in addition to a lengthened "school day" the children require 24-hour supervision. Adequate numbers of adults for a field trip to the natural history museum will seem far too slim at about 11 P.M. on the first night.

You will need to get commitments from those who are willing to be your staff members and get them early. Because the ROE schedule can be demanding of time, talents, and energy, it is important to let all members of your staff know precisely when and what responsibilities they will have, and train them with respect to such duties and responsibilities. This is particularly true if you plan on using parents or high school students as chaperons.

Even teachers need some extra help if they are to take on the resident experience. Research suggests that most teachers do not feel confident teaching in the outdoors. Arranging for training sessions, at the ROE site preferably, will reduce the inevitable anxieties. If a training program is not feasible, arrange for less experienced teachers to observe the more experienced ones before taking over a particular lesson. Being able to watch a model lesson often fills in the holes much more effectively than simply receiving a written lesson plan.

Schedules. As you begin your planning process, you will quickly realize that you have far more to accomplish than you have time to accomplish it in. Work with your staff to develop a detailed plan which names the students in each group, what each will do, and who will supervise the activity, hour by hour, from the time buses load until they return and unload. Many of those who provide ROE experiences have developed forms they use in this process (see sample schedule form). Some of the facilities even provide planning handbooks for schools to help guide teachers in planning. There is no reason to exclude students from this process—quite the contrary. Bear in mind that the more one involves the staff and students in planning, the more it becomes "their program." As you begin this phase of your planning process, you will need to make some basic decisions about how you arrange the schedule: How many students will you have in a learning group? Will learning groups remain the same throughout the entire experience? Will one or two adults spend the entire time with the same group of 10 to 20 students, or will you rotate your staff among the students? Likewise, decisions must be made about dormitory, dining hall, and table setting assignments.

Some instructors like to use a very tight, detailed schedule when conducting ROE experiences. They like to have things nailed down and to know well in advance what will take place where and when. Others prefer to work from an outline, plan as they go along, and take advantage of whatever comes up. Using a very flexible schedule, they do much pupil–teacher planning and work independently of others.

No matter how the students are divided or whether or not the program is tightly planned or not, a basic schedule must be devised. In reality, the schedule will revolve around meal, bed, and rising times. If you control your own meals (i.e., you cook them yourselves), you have a great deal of flexibility. But most ROE centers have set meal times which, in essence, define your program periods. It is probably easiest to think about the program schedule as starting with loading the bus back at your school on the day of departure. With arrival at the ROE center being somewhat before noon, much of the time before lunch will be spent on settling in, orientation, and awareness activities. About an hour is allowed for lunch, and this is followed by instructional

Sample Schedule Form

Time	Day	Time	Day	Time	Day
School _____ ROE Staff _____ Dates _____					
Students & Grade _____ _____ _____					
			Table setters: ____ _____ Breakfast		Table setters: ____ _____ Breakfast
	Table setters: ____ _____ Lunch		Table setters: ____ _____ Lunch		Table setters: ____ _____ Lunch *Notes:*
	Table setters: ____ _____ Dinner		Table setters: ____ _____ Dinner		

activities that run until about an hour before dinner. Evening activities continue according to the age of the students—perhaps as late as 10:00 P.M. for upper-grade students. Subsequent days have about the same pattern, except that on the last day, time should be provided for packing up, cleaning, and reviewing the experience. Most leaders attempt to leave the ROE site so that they arrive back at school shortly before the regular dismissal time so that the buses can make their regular runs.

Staff at ROE facilities seem to prefer longer blocks of time for their activities, with a full morning or afternoon for a particular activity or combination of activities. Many teachers who are participating in ROE for the first time or two prefer shorter periods of 1½ hours or so. The person in charge of coordinating or scheduling should keep this in mind and attempt to accommodate both, letting the ROE staff members have back-to-back sessions with their groups of students.

Approvals. Get the approval of school administrators. Do this early because in some school districts approval for activities of this nature comes only from the board of education. Then present the idea to the children's parents, involve them, and get their support. Once the idea becomes established in the community and/or school, such approvals become routine, but until such time, ROE is looked upon as an extraordinary undertaking requiring discussion at the highest levels. Parents should, of course, be required to sign the appropriate permission forms, liability waivers, and medical history and treatment forms several weeks before the dates set for the big adventure. Once you have a schedule in place and have a better idea of the types of activities you will offer during the ROE experience, conduct a "parent meeting" in which you review your plans with parents. If at all possible, show the parents slides or a video tape of the ROE site, with visual examples of the types of experiences in which the children will participate, including shots of the dormitory, dining hall, and grounds.

Site/Facility. Arrange for the use of your chosen site. Specify the dates, costs, numbers to be included, and services to be provided. If unclear, visit the site to discuss your program and needs. Keep in touch with staff at the site. Contracts may require the signature of someone in the school's administration hierarchy.

Transportation. There have been a few cases in which everyone was in the parking lot but no bus arrived; someone forgot to arrange for transportation. Just be sure to check and recheck ahead of time to ensure that the person responsible did order the bus (or buses) and that the bus company did not lose the order. Also, check for the return trip! Although a rare occurrence, drivers have been known to have difficulty in finding the school or the campsite. You might want to help by giving specific directions.

ROE as a Model for Learning and Living

One of the major goals of the ROE experience is to promote environmental understandings and appreciation. Throughout the ROE experience it will be important to model, for the children, environmentally responsible behaviors. Simple but important expectations concerning staying on trails, care of plants, and consideration of wildlife must be communicated to the children. It follows that the ROE facility and its management should advance this goal as much as possible also. Consequently, as you select and use a particular site, questions concerning the environmental standards of the facility should be asked. To that end, the following is intended as a partial listing of environmental concerns and questions. Does the center or site:

Solid Waste:

   Have a recycling program?

   Maintain a compost pile?

   Use post-consumer recycled paper in the office? . . . in the dining hall? . . . in the dormitory
   bathrooms?

   Collect "lost and found" clothing items and re-use, if those items are not claimed by their
   owners?

Energy:

   Use high-efficiency light bulbs wherever possible?

   Have well-insulated buildings?

   Use storm windows and doors where appropriate?

   Set the thermostats at appropriate energy-saving temperatures day and night?

   For outdoor lighting, use a mechanism (e.g. motion detector) so that lighting is only on when
   needed?

   Use solar power, where feasible, for outdoor lighting?

   Install timers or other mechanisms in classrooms so that lights will automatically go out when
   the room is not in use?

   Post energy saving reminders at light switches and near doors?

   Use "human powered" machines rather than gas or electric ones (e.g. leaf blowers)?

   Use solar water heaters for at least some of the hot water uses?

Water:

   Install low-flow shower heads and toilets?

   Post water conservation reminders near water facets?

   Fix dripping faucets?

   Provide information concerning the source of the drinking water and how water and sewage
   is disposed?

Management of the Grounds:

Keep trails in repair to avoid erosion?

Use native plants in landscaping, keeping use of non-native species to an absolute minimum?

Protect environmentally sensitive areas, limiting use of particularly fragile areas?

Maintain a picking policy for plant materials?

Maintain policies that protect animals from harassment, especially during mating season?

Dining Hall:

Use cloth napkins? If this is not feasible, are 100 percent post-consumer recycled napkins used?

Offer an option for vegetarian meals?

Use non-disposable dishes and utensils?

Maintain a food waste program that weighs and charts the amount of food thrown away at each meal?

Allow participants to regulate the amount of food put on their own plate?

The resident outdoor education program, if planned properly, can become the centerpiece of students' educational experiences. There is no mystery to the success of ROE programs, but all will agree that the experience is magical.

RI

7

2011

3

5

5

05 2010